The Little Logic Book

The Little Logic Book

Lee Hardy
Del Ratzsch
Rebecca Konyndyk DeYoung
Gregory Mellema

The CALVIN
COLLEGE PRESS

Grand Rapids, Michigan • calvincollegepress.com

Published 2013 by the Calvin College Press
3201 Burton St. SE
Grand Rapids, MI 49546

Printed in the United States of America

Publisher's Cataloging-in-Publication Data

Hardy, Lee, 1950-
    The Little logic book / Lee Hardy , Del Ratzsch , Rebecca Konyndyk DeYoung , Gregory Mellema.
    p. cm.
    ISBN 978-1-937555-10-8

1. Logic --Problems, exercises, etc. 2. Reasoning. 3. Analogy. 4. Fallacies (Logic). 5. Probabilities. 6. Induction (Logic). 7. Explanation. I. Ratzsch, Delvin Lee, 1945-. II. DeYoung, Rebecca Konyndyk, 1971-. III. Mellema, Gregory, 1948-. IV. Title..

BC71 .H235 2013
160/.76 --dc23   2013947744

Cover design: Lee Hardy
Cover background image: iStockphoto

Table of Contents

Preface

Does the world need another logic text? Clearly, we think so.

The idea for the text you're reading grew out of some frustration we had in finding a supplementary logic text for our Introduction to Philosophy classes at Calvin College that combined three features in addition to providing coverage of the basic points in logic: first, affordability; second, some ethical reflection on the use of logic in argumentation; third, a balanced treatment of religious belief in the examples and exercises.

On the affordability score, we elected to publish with the Calvin College Press in order to maintain some control over the price of the text. In addition, we have decided to put the logic exercises for each chapter in free downloadable PDF files (for the files go to calvincollegepress.com). This arrangement allows us to update the exercises periodically without publishing new editions, since the latter practice undercuts the value of used copies of the text. Of course, we firmly believe that most students will want to make this text a part of their permanent personal library, but we realize that some of them might reluctantly agree to sell their copies out of concern for the poor among us and that the availability of used and usable textbooks makes education more affordable for all.

In the ethics department, we decided to include a chapter at the end of the book devoted to exploring the ethics of argument. There we discuss the main purpose of constructing and assessing arguments, the attitudes we maintain toward the people who serve as our partners in dialogue and the positions they represent, the practices we engage in when we debate an issue, and the propensities those practices form within us. We're sticking with words that start with *p* here to facilitate memory. Given the sad state of civil discourse in our culture, we hope this chapter will be considered just as important as the chapters on the more technical aspects of logic.

On the third point, we have discovered to our dismay—but not to our surprise—a definite antireligious bias in many of the supplementary logic texts on offer today. One might think that logic, a formal discipline, is a religiously neutral subject if ever there was one. After all, the deductive argument form modus ponens is the same for everyone, regardless of religious perspective. But the teaching and practice of logic are always carried out in larger contexts, contexts informed, ultimately, by larger convictions. In logic texts those convictions often surface in the examples and exercises. In the three supplementary logic books I have used in my Introduction to Philosophy class to date, one can find no instance where a religious belief appears in a logically favorable light: Jesus's statement that "you are either for me or against me" is cited in two of the books as an example of a false dichotomy; the belief in a Creator God stands as the conclusion of a bad analogical argument; the resistance to grand evolutionary theory is portrayed as the result of a religious person's refusal to consider contrary evidence; a minister's advice to married couples to share devotional time in order to improve their marriage as a result of causal oversimplification; the conviction that one should start going to church again to avoid yet another financial disaster as a case of the post hoc fallacy; a religious objection to dance because dance was once a pagan practice as an example of the genetic fallacy; a family's appeal to a son to stick with his church as a case of unwarranted appeal to tradition. Two of the three books I used did take theological stands, suggesting that reports of miracles in the Bible are not essential to the Christian faith. An expanded review we sponsored of ten of the most often used introductory logic and critical thinking textbooks revealed a pattern consistent with my smaller sample. A total of 160 references to religious beliefs were identified. Of them, 64 were judged to be neutral, 6 were positive, and 90 were negative. One of the texts on critical thinking contained 42 religious references, 14 were neutral, 28 were negative, and none were positive. Of course, religious beliefs are sometimes supported by bad arguments. But they are also sometimes supported by good arguments. The latter, however, are rather dramatically underrepresented in logic texts on the market today. Reading them, one might easily gather the impression that reason and religion are inherently opposed. We try to take a more balanced approach in this text, recognizing that fallacious reasoning can show up in both the religious and the antireligious camps. It's an equal opportunity employer.

There are several other ways this text distinguishes itself from the standard fare in logic textbooks. Most of the chapters start with a dialogue—usually a heated debate—between three college students on some social, philosophical, or religious issue. Embedded in each dialogue is the mode of reasoning we wish take up, describe, and comment on in the rest of the chapter. We have adopted this device because we want to remind ourselves and our readers that logic is not the exclusive property of professional logicians. We all make use of a variety of argument forms, often without an explicit awareness of the rules we are following—or violating—just as we make use of grammatical rules in the course of speaking without an explicit awareness of doing so. Grammarians isolate and codify those rules; logicians do something similar in the case of the rules of reasoning (although we think that logic is more than just a matter of codifying conventions).

Second, there is a fair amount of philosophical commentary on the modes of reasoning treated in the chapters. The text is designed to be used as a supplementary text in philosophy courses, and thus less emphasis is placed on the acquisition of logical techniques. We hope the philosophical commentary will contribute to class discussion of the assumptions and implications of various kinds of reasoning we humans engage in.

Third, the text includes both more and less content than many of its peers. It is not intended to support a semester-long course in logic. For that purpose, one should make use of a solid 600-page logic text that pulls in all sides of the forms of logic discussed, provides extensive examples and exercises, sidebars, historical asides, and the like. Much of that is lacking in this text. We do not include a review of Aristotelian logic, Venn diagrams, or even natural deduction techniques. What we do provide is a core of concepts, distinctions, explanations, rules of inference, methods of assessment, and examples that will allow students to get their feet wet and deal with texts and issues in a philosophy class with a greater degree of logical sophistication. Because of this spare approach, we do not claim that this text is pedagogically self-sufficient. We think it can be read with benefit by anyone with an interest in logic, but its success as a textbook will depend less on our brilliant writing than on the genius of the instructor at hand. We provide an entrée and the basic information, which in turn should serve as a platform for the instructor, who will explain and expand on the text according to the needs of students and the demands of the course. That's as it should be, actually. It is our intent to enter into a team-teaching effort, not to convert the professor into a mere teaching assistant.

That said, we also cover more topics than most introductory logic texts include. We have chapters on modal logic, counterfactuals, and probability theory. Such topics are usually reserved for intermediate and advanced logic courses. But we note that these argument forms are often employed in everyday discourse, and so we think they belong in a text meant to cover the typical ways in which we in fact reason with each other. The table of contents, then, should be seen more as a menu than as a sequence for a step-by-step path through the entire thicket of basic logic. Introduction to Philosophy classes may want to make use of just the chapters on deduction, induction, analogical arguments, informal fallacies, Mill's methods, explanation, and the ethics of argument. A course in the philosophy of religion may want to pick up the chapters on modal logic, probability, and scientific inference; a course in the philosophy of science might choose deduction, induction, analogical arguments, Mill's methods, explanation, and scientific inference.

We have enjoyed the support of our colleagues and our college in the writing of this book. We would like to thank our colleagues in the Department of Philosophy at Calvin College who reviewed much of our work in our legendary Tuesday department colloquia. We would like to thank the Kuyers Institute of Teaching and Learning at Calvin College for grant support and its director, David Smith, for his encouragement. Susan Felch, Executive Editor of the Calvin College Press, is also to be mentioned for her support and sage advice. Beyond our department, we are thankful for reviews of an earlier version of the manuscript from Dean Ward and Elizabeth Vander Lei (English), Garth Pauley (Communication Arts and Sciences), and philosophy and English double major Trenton Heille. Calvin graduate and now philosophy graduate student Emi Okayasu helped us with a review of other logic texts on the market. A good dozen other colleagues, spread across the globe, have favored us as well with their comments on our project.

Finally, here's to the culinary tour Del Ratzsch and I took of the restaurants and delis of Ada, Michigan, as we labored over the strategies, details, and phrasings of the final version of this text.

Lee Hardy
General Editor, on behalf of the authors

1.

Deductive Arguments

Like most late-night philosophical wrangles in the dorm, the discussion in Andrea's room was making no progress whatever. René just *knew* that what made humans so unique was that each of us has a nonphysical, immaterial, even spiritual, soul or mind that is the center of our thinking, the core of our consciousness, the part of us that makes us who we are, the *real* self. And just as firmly, Andrea *knew* that we were purely physical, biological beings—marvelously complex, conscious, thinking biological beings, but purely physical nonetheless. To this point, their attempts to convince each other had predictably failed.

Just then Andrea's roommate Melissa stumbled in. It was pretty obvious that despite being underage, Melissa had been into something a little stronger than her usual Diet Pepsi. Exasperated, Andrea turned Melissa into Exhibit A for her position on the physical nature of human beings:

> Look: if what passes for Melissa's thinking occurred in some *non*physical part of her, a mind or soul or something, then alcohol, which is absolutely and completely *physical*, couldn't have any effect on it. But it's pretty obvious that alcohol *has* totally messed up her mind—oops, she just passed out. Just leave her there on the floor—she'll sleep it off. Now where was I? Oh, right—so whatever it is that does her thinking can't be some spooky, nonphysical ghostly thing—a mind or a soul or whatever. That *proves* I'm right.

René, however, wasn't convinced. And Melissa? She just kept snoring.

I. Arguments: Basic Concepts

Any attempt, such as Andrea's, to establish a position by giving reasons for it is an **argument**. Arguments are among the primary intellectual tools we use both in everyday life and in academic contexts. Rarely do we just stake out positions—abortion is wrong, global warming is occurring, premarital sex is OK, everyone who is kind will go to heaven, the cosmos is over 14 billion years old, food preservatives are harmful, Iran is a sponsor of terrorism, the Cubs are going to lose this year, aliens abducted my brother-in-law, Starbucks coffee is wildly overpriced, my philosophy professor is awesome, evolutionary theory explains biodiversity, Napoleon was a lousy strategist—and expect everyone around us to abandon their views without ceremony and embrace ours merely on our say-so. Instead, we try to convince others by giving arguments. That's true in academic journals, in the classroom, around the dinner table, on the Internet, and in the residence hall.

Arguments, however, are not just tools for persuading others of views we think are true or dissuading them from views we think are false. Sometimes we're not sure if a view is true or false, so we cast about to see if there are any good arguments for or against it. Arguments can serve as tools for discovering the truth as well as tools for defending what we already think is true, or for criticizing what we already think is false.

More precisely, we can say that an argument is a set of statements that consists of **premises** and a **conclusion**. The conclusion is the position one wishes to establish, support, or defend. Premises are the claims, principles, or alleged facts cited in support of the conclusion. They are the statements from which the conclusion is supposed to follow—from which one is to *reason* to the conclusion.

Some arguments are very good. Other arguments leave a lot to be desired. Clearly, if we care about knowing the truth and making decisions based on reality, we need to be able to sort the good from the bad. Otherwise we may find ourselves taken in by serious error, duped by the faulty arguments of various political, religious, ideological, and commercial con artists. Moreover, without the ability to assess arguments, we run the risk of rejecting important truths or accepting falsehoods because of our own errors in reasoning.

But how do we distinguish good arguments from bad? How do we determine whether or not we should be convinced by a specific argument? As it turns out, the defining components of arguments—premises and conclusions—generate two key questions for the assessment of an argument's strength:

1. Do the premises in fact *logically support* the conclusion?
2. Are the premises in fact *true*?

If the premises of an argument are in fact true, and *if* the premises in fact logically support the conclusion, then the argument constitutes good grounds for accepting the conclusion. Determining the answers to 1 and 2 is thus essential in the assessment of arguments. Arguments that fail on one or the other—or both—of those counts have the potential to lead us astray. Whether or not we should believe a conclusion, whether we should act on that conclusion, whether that conclusion should lead us to alter some previous deeply held belief—the answers to these questions may be riding on the answers to 1 and 2.

It is important to recognize that the two questions are, strictly speaking, independent of each other. Suppose that Andrea mentions to René that she just spent $95 on a great phone deal. Melissa (having just awakened and regained her senses) says that she got the same phone for $45. René naturally infers that Melissa spent less than Andrea, and she has drawn the right conclusion from what she has been told. Her reasoning here is flawless. But in fact Melissa was just trying to impress René—she actually spent $120. The premises René had to work with did in fact logically lead to the conclusion she drew, giving a positive answer to question 1. But she was reasoning from a premise that was not actually true, giving a negative answer to question 2.

It is also important to recognize that if an argument fails either question 1 or 2, or both, that fact alone does not tell us whether the conclusion of the argument is true or false. The failure of 1 tells us merely that the premises do not adequately support the conclusion. But the conclusion might still be true. The failure of 2 tells us only that the argument involves reasoning from at least one false premise. But again, the conclusion might still be true. In fact, an argument that fails on *both* counts may still have a true conclusion. All we can say in those situations is that the argument does not provide us with a good reason to accept the conclusion. It does not tell us whether the conclusion itself is true.

So far, so good. But how do we get answers to those two key questions, answers that will help us decide if we have a good reason to accept a conclusion? With respect to question 2, the question of the truth of the premises, the answer will depend on what the premises are. To determine the truth of an argument's premises we might have to check historical facts, the results of biological research, matters of common sense, population statistics—it depends on what the argument is about. Our investigations will be as wide-ranging as the topics of the arguments we are assessing.

The situation with question 1, the question of how well the premises support the conclusion, is very different. Here philosophy gives us a hand. Distinguishing good reasoning from bad reasoning—in short, answering question 1—is the primary focus of the philosophical subdiscipline of **logic**. Logic does not concern itself with whether the premises of an argument are true; it deals exclusively with what we could correctly infer from a set of premises *if* they were true.

Logic, then, does not cover everything that makes for a good argument. It doesn't pronounce on the truth of the premises or the conclusion (unless they are true because they are **tautologies** or false because they are **contradictions**). It only tell us if the conclusion follows from the premises of a proposed argument.

There is an additional virtue of arguments that largely falls outside the scope of logic. When we give an argument, we often are attempting to convince our audience of the truth of a certain proposition. It is entirely possible for us to construct an argument that comes out OK on question 2 because the premises are in fact true, and comes out OK on question 1 because the premises do indeed support the conclusion—and yet we still fail to convince our audience. Somehow we failed to read our listeners. We used premises they find wildly implausible; we embarked on a course of reasoning that utterly mystifies them; we offended them in the way we put the point; we dealt with an issue about which they don't even care enough to form an opinion; we assumed they were open to argument when in fact they were not. Our argument was logically flawless, but it failed to persuade. It was, we can say, rhetorically unsuccessful. The study of what makes for successful persuasion is pursued in the discipline of rhetoric, which is separate from the discipline of logic. Even so, in a discussion of logic it is important to consider how we use arguments in our attempts to persuade others, how we relate to others in the course of giving arguments for what we believe is true (or against what we think is false), and so a number of issues that point us beyond logic are brought up in the final chapter of this book on the ethics of argument.

II. Deductive Arguments: Concept and Definition

The logical support that premises give to a conclusion can come in different degrees: from none at all to weak to strong to absolutely conclusive. We can distinguish different categories of argument in terms of those degrees. The most powerful arguments, logically speaking, are found in the deductive category. **Deductive arguments** are arguments in which the premises are intended to provide logically ironclad support for the conclusion. They claim that if their premises are true, the conclusion has to be true. In many areas, however, our evidence cannot provide that kind of support for a conclusion; at best it can provide only strong partial support. Arguments where we aim at establishing that the conclusion is probable are categorized as non-deductive arguments (sometimes the term *inductive arguments* is used to cover all non-deductive arguments). Those arguments are discussed in other chapters of this text.

If a deductive argument successfully fulfills the deductive intent—if the premises actually do provide logically ironclad support for the conclusion—then the argument is said to be deductively *valid*. A deductively valid argument is one that meets the following condition:

> **Valid₁:** It is *not logically possible* for all the premises of the argument to be true and for the conclusion of the argument to be false at the same time.

Another way of saying exactly the same thing is:

> **Valid₂:** It is *logically necessary* that if all the premises of the argument are true, then the conclusion of the argument is true as well.

Any deductive argument that fails to meet the condition of validity is **invalid**. In ordinary conversation the term valid is often used to indicate that a proposition, principle, position, or point made is reasonable, true, or especially relevant (e.g., "That's a valid point."). In logic, however, the term is used exclusively according to the definitions given above. Only arguments are valid or invalid. Likewise, we here reserve the terms *true* and *false* to describe the status of statements: only statements are true or false.

In logic we also make a distinction between valid and **sound** deductive arguments. In terms of the two key questions, a sound argument is one where

1. the argument is deductively valid; and
2. all the premises of the argument are in fact true.

Since those two conditions together guarantee that the conclusion of a sound argument will also be true, sound arguments are sometimes referred to as **proofs**. A proposed proof will fail if it is not deductively valid or if one or more of the premises is in fact false, or—worse yet—if it violates both conditions, arguing invalidly from false premises. Again, the fact that an argument fails one or both of the conditions for being a proof does not automatically mean that the conclusion of the argument is false. Moreover, the failure of an argument to measure up to the requirements of a rigorous proof does not automatically mean that the argument is unimportant, of little value, or anything of the sort. In many areas, the best arguments we have are not proofs.

III. Determining Validity and Invalidity

Usually—but not always—the validity of a deductive argument is determined by its **form**. By "form" we mean the pattern of logical relationships among the components of an argument's premises and conclusion. Here is a simple example:

> If you fail to get a job this summer,
>> then you won't be able to pay tuition next fall.
> If you won't be able to pay tuition next fall,
>> then you will have to drop out of school next year.
> So: If you fail to get a job this summer,
>> then you will have to drop out of school next year.

As you can see, several statements appear more than once in this argument. Just to make the overall logical pattern in that argument clearer, we'll use letters to represent the statements involved:

- The letter *A* will represent the statement "You fail to get a job this summer."
- The letter *B* will represent the statement "You won't be able to pay tuition next fall."
- The letter *C* will represent the statement "You will have to drop out of school next year."

Using those letters, the argument now looks like this:

	1. If *A* then *B*.	(Or:	If *A* is true, then *B* is true.
	2. If *B* then *C*.		If *B* is true, then *C* is true.
So:	3. If *A* then *C*.	So:	If *A* is true, then *C* is true.)

We can now easily see the logical form of the argument. That particular form even has its own name: hypothetical syllogism (usually abbreviated HS). And if we think carefully about that form, we can see that the argument is deductively valid: if *A* gets us to *B*, and *B* gets us to *C*, it follows that by starting with *A* we will get to *C*. Those premises lead us inevitably to the conclusion. If the premises are true, the conclusion has to be true. And that is what deductive validity amounts to: once we accept the premises, the conclusion is logically inescapable.

By the same token we can see that *any* argument in the form of a hypothetical syllogism, no matter what the topic, no matter what the content of the premises, will be deductively valid. If we begin a piece of reasoning with two premises like 1 and 2, and infer a conclusion corresponding to 3, our reasoning will be flawless. We don't need to know whether the premises are true or not. Indeed, we don't even have to understand the premises. So long as the argument has that form—HS—it is a deductively valid argument; the reasoning it embodies is ironclad.

Being able to recognize the form of deductive arguments is a very handy skill when it comes to evaluating their logical validity. Conveniently enough, there are a limited number of basic deductive argument forms. Once we identify them, we can tell instantly from the form alone if the argument before us is deductively valid. The following are the most common valid forms. Long recognized, their names have historical roots. The letters A, B, and C below can stand for any statement, fact, principle, proposition, belief, or supposition.

Modus Ponens (MP)	**Modus Tollens (MT)**
If *A* then *B*.	If *A* then *B*.
A.	*B* is not true.
Therefore,	Therefore,
B.	*A* is not true.

Disjunctive Syllogism (DS)	Hypothetical Syllogism (HS)
Either *A* or *B*.	If *A* then *B*.
B is not true.	If *B* then *C*.
Therefore,	Therefore,
A.	If *A* then *C*.

Just as with HS, if you think carefully about the other argument forms above, you should be able to see that in each case if the premises were true, the conclusion would be inescapable—in short, you should be able to see that they are deductively valid forms. For instance, modus ponens simply says that if one thing leads to a second thing, then establishing the first guarantees the second. The disjunctive syllogism tells us the obvious truth that if there are a limited number of options, then ruling out all but one guarantees the truth of the one remaining.

In everyday conversation and debate, arguments are not always stated straightforwardly in easily recognizable forms. There are many stylistic variants, and different contexts can make different presentations appropriate. Sometimes a speaker or author will first give us the conclusion she is aiming at, then lay out premises in support of that conclusion. Since we already know what the conclusion is, that sequence can make it easier to see the relevance of the premises as they are presented. Sometimes we'll be given some of the premises, then the conclusion, then the remaining premises. Sometimes the conclusion will come at the very end. Sometimes one (or more) of the premises will not even be explicitly stated. An argument with an unstated premise is called an **enthymeme**. Enthymemes often occur when a premise is obvious, not in dispute, or already an explicit part of the discussion. Sometimes enthymemes occur because the unstated premise is so bizarre or implausible that bringing it out into the open would instantly discredit the entire argument. Arguments with unstated conclusions are called enthymemes as well. Sometimes the conclusion to be drawn so obviously follows from the premises that it need not be explicitly stated. It goes without saying.

Arguments as stated, then, may not be easy to evaluate. When we are evaluating an argument, trying to identify its form in order to assess its validity, we customarily put the argument in a conventional form with all the premises—stated or unstated—explicitly listed and numbered in order one by one, with the conclusion explicitly stated at the end.

Now recall Andrea's argument at the beginning of this chapter. In conventional form the core of her argument looks like this:

1. *If* Melissa's thinking occurs in a nonphysical mind or soul *then* her thinking would be unaffected by alcohol.
2. It is not true that her thinking is unaffected by alcohol.

Therefore,

3. It is not true that Melissa's thinking occurs in a nonphysical mind or soul.

This argument is an instance of the modus tollens form. Thus it is deductively valid (an answer to question 1 above). Of course, there is still the question of whether the premises are in fact true (question 2), and René—or you—might wish to challenge one of the premises, most likely the first premise.

There are also variations on some of the basic argument forms. For instance, two valid forms—constructive dilemma and destructive dilemma—are a sort of double-barreled modus ponens and a double-barreled modus tollens respectively:

Constructive Dilemma (CD)

If A then B.
If C then D.
Either A is true
    or C is true.
Therefore,
Either B is true
    or D is true.

Destructive Dilemma (DD)

If A then B.
If C then D.
Either B is false
    or D is false.
Therefore,
Either A is false
    or C is false.

There are some very common invalid deductive argument forms as well. These are also known as deductive fallacies, and it is important to be able to recognize them. The two most frequently encountered are these:

Affirming the Consequent (AC)

If A then B.
B is true.
Therefore,
A is true.

Denying the Antecedent (DA)

If A then B.
A is not true.
Therefore,
B is not true.

In conditional statements ("If A then B") the first statement (A) is the **antecedent**, the second statement (B) is the **consequent**. In each of these arguments involving conditional statements, it is possible for the premises to be true while the conclusion is false, thus violating the definition of validity. Here is an example of the **fallacy** of affirming the consequent (where the consequent of the first premise is affirmed in the second premise):

> 1. If Queen Elizabeth were president of the United States, then she would be very well-known.
> 2. Queen Elizabeth is very well-known.
>
> Therefore,
> 3. Queen Elizabeth is president of the United States.

Both of the premises are true, but the conclusion is not—rather unfortunately, since Elizabeth seems to be way more sensible and classy than most of our current politicians. Clearly there are many reasons why Queen Elizabeth could be very well-known. Being president of the United States would be only one of them. Thus the fact that she is very well-known does not prove that she is the president of the United States. She could also be very well-known because she was the Queen of England or a popular British rapper.

It is important to see that arguments of this form (AC) are invalid even if the conclusion is true. Here's another example. Suppose that René had done so well in her organic chem class last semester that her professor told her she would get an A for the semester if she got 93 or above on the final exam. So it's obviously true that

> 1. If René gets a 97 on her final exam, she gets an A for the semester.

And in fact it turned out that

> 2. René did get an A for the semester.

We might well be tempted to infer that

> Therefore,
> 3. René got a 97 on her final exam.

But that doesn't necessarily follow. Maybe René got a 93, or 94, or 95, or 96, or 98, or 99, or maybe even 100. In any of those cases, both premises (1) and (2) would *still* have been true—but the conclusion would have been false. So it is logically possible for premises (1) and (2) to be true, but for the conclusion (3) to be false, and that meets the definition of an invalid argument. As it turns out, René did get a 97 on her final exam, so the conclusion (3) is in fact true. Nonetheless, the argument is still invalid. Despite the fact that the conclusion happens to be true in this case, it does not follow logically from the premises. Premises (1) and (2) do not logically guarantee that (3) is true.

IV. Connectives and Symbols

You may also have noticed that the words *if* and *then* occur several times in the various argument forms, linking two statements together. Terms that make more complex statements out of simple statements are called **connectives**. Here are some common connectives and their standard symbols:

Connective	Read	Often Symbolized	
Conjunction	Both A and B	$A \wedge B$	(or $A \cdot B$)
Disjunction	Either A or B	$A \vee B$	
Conditional	If A then B	$A \rightarrow B$	(or $A \supset B$)
Biconditional	A if and only if B	$A \equiv B$	
Negation	Not A*	$\sim A$	(or $\neg A$)

*There are several alternative phrases for negation: e.g., A is not true, A is false, it is not the case that A.

There are two more symbols in addition to the symbols used for connectives that help us represent the logic of an argument. A capital letter from the alphabet is used to symbolize a simple proposition. A simple proposition like "René got a 97 on her exam," for instance, can be symbolized simply by the letter A. We also use a three-dot symbol (here used with a slash: / ∴) as a conclusion indicator. It stands for "Therefore."

We can symbolyze modus ponens and disjunctive syllogism respectively as

$$A \rightarrow B \qquad\qquad A \vee B$$
$$A \qquad\qquad\qquad \sim B$$
$$/ \therefore B \qquad\qquad / \therefore A$$

VII. Complex Deductive Arguments

A large proportion of the arguments that we encounter in everyday life or philosophy are not deductive arguments. Instead, they are inductive, analogical, probabilistic, and so forth. Those kinds of arguments are discussed elsewhere in this text. Of the deductive arguments that are of some significance, most are far more complex than the simple forms introduced above. Indeed, some are so complex that it's hard to tell whether they are deductively valid.

Complex deductive arguments are built up of simple arguments. If we define an **inference** as the mental move we make from the premises of an argument to its conclusion, we can say that complex arguments contain more than one inference. Complex arguments, then, need to be evaluated in steps; their basic arguments need to be considered individually. Consider how Melissa might attempt to come to the rescue of René's belief in the soul with the following complex argument:

> René is right that we have immaterial minds and souls, and here's the proof. If people did have immaterial parts like that, then people could obviously have immaterial, mystical experiences. And that is really true. Lots of people *do* have such experiences, not only great saints but sometimes even perfectly ordinary people. Jason's uncle has had lots of experiences his doctor can't explain. And if medical science can't explain something, then it has to involve some higher level of reality—and that's mystical.

Melissa has given an argument for the view that we have immaterial minds or souls, and that argument contains a subargument in support of the key premise that some people do indeed have mystical experiences. Subarguments for key premises are common when the premise in question is unfamiliar, controversial, or thought to need support for some other reason. Here, in simplified form, is the overall structure of Melissa's argument:

1. If people have immaterial minds or souls, then some people could have immaterial, mystical experiences.

   Subargument:
   a. If science cannot explain a specific experience, then that experience is mystical.

    b. Some people (like Jason's uncle) have experiences science
       cannot explain.
Subconclusion:
Therefore,
    c. Some people have immaterial, mystical experiences.

The subconclusion (c) will now function as premise (2) in the
main argument:

    2. Some people have immaterial, mystical experiences.
Therefore,
    3. People have immaterial minds or souls.

In the subargument, (a) and (b) lead to a subconclusion (c) that then
functions as premise (2) in the main argument, where (1) and (2) lead to
the conclusion (3). Note that the subargument is a type of modus ponens
inference, which is valid. But unfortunately the main argument commits
the fallacy of affirming the consequent, which is invalid. Coming from
Melissa, that may not be too surprising.

V. Summary and Conclusion

Deductive arguments are logically powerful arguments. In fact, they are
the most powerful arguments we have at our disposal. Not only are they
useful in many contexts; in some circumstances they can be absolutely
decisive. Historically they have been seen as having a crucial role in governing our beliefs and in defining what it means for humans to be rational. Some philosophers have even argued that we only really *know* those
things for which we have deductive proofs. After all, if we have a deductive proof for something, then we are *guaranteed* that it is true. And
many have thought that such guarantees are what genuine knowledge
requires. Although nearly all philosophers now reject that view (and you
might want to examine the arguments on which they base that rejection),
deductive proofs are nice when we can get them.

There are many areas of human life, however, where we simply do
not have knock-down, drag-out deductive arguments. In those areas,
we must rely on other sources and means of identifying truth, guarding
against errors, governing our beliefs, directing our actions, and persuading others. But sharpening the deductive components of our reasoning

abilities can help keep us on track in those tasks wherever deductive reasoning applies. That sharpening may be difficult. But it is also crucial. Perhaps a bit more logic would have helped Melissa to avoid the logical mistake she made earlier. On the other hand, helping her avoid some of her behavioral mistakes may take a little more work.

2.

Truth Tables

The news just updated on the CNN website. The lifeless body of a child that had been abducted a week ago was discovered by the edge of a rural highway. The Amber Alert was called off. The hunt for the male suspect was still on.

"He does, Andrea! He *absolutely* deserves to die, a scum like that. I mean, he abducts a defenseless child, and then leaves it to die by the side of a road. In fact, mere death is way too good for that kind of vermin." René was practically spitting fire.

"OK—suppose you're right. And maybe you are." This from Andrea. "I'm certainly not about to defend him or the horrible things he did. But even if death is what he deserves, that doesn't mean that *we* have the right to murder him."

"Murder?! Who's talking about *murder*? I'm talking about capital punishment."

"So am I. *Any* killing of another person is murder. What the motivation might be, or who is doing it, doesn't make any difference. Killing is murder."

"But it isn't murder when a government does it. That's why it's called capital *punishment*."

"Oh, right." Andrea's voice was edged with sarcasm. "I suppose that just because the Nazis were the government that their slaughter of Jews wasn't murder? Or Stalin's extermination of millions of people? Or Pol Pot's lethal campaigns in Cambodia? Or South American government death squads? Or state-sponsored terrorism? A lynch mob is still committing murder even if it's led by a sheriff."

"That's different. I'm talking about when a proper, legitimate government is acting strictly according to law."

"You want things according to law? OK, fine. What about the Constitution forbidding cruel and unusual punishment? It doesn't get much more cruel than depriving someone of their life. But that's exactly what capital punishment does. So capital punishment is unconstitutional, and that makes it murder even by your definition."

"Oh, come on, Andrea. It says cruel *and* unusual punishment. The term is *'and,'* Andrea—*'and.'* By definition that means *both*. I don't think it actually is cruel when it's deserved, like in this case. But even if it were cruel, the prohibition is on punishment that is cruel *and* unusual—being cruel is only one of the two conditions that have to be met for it to be forbidden."

"No, that's not what 'and' means here. What it means is that cruel punishment is forbidden *and, moreover,* unusual punishment is forbidden too."

"I don't believe this," an exasperated Melissa finally weighed in. "We're talking about what should happen to a slimeball who could do what he did to that child, and you guys end up squabbling over definitions again. Forget the definitions—that's just semantics, who cares? I'll tell you what should actually happen to that guy in the *real* world. Somebody should just take a baseball bat and . . ."

"Yeah, yeah, we know what your solution is, Melissa," interrupted René, thereby depriving us and all future generations of knowing Melissa's solution.

I. Connectives

In the previous chapter on deduction, a number of basic connectives were introduced: conjunctions ("and"), disjunctions ("either . . . or"), negations ("not"), conditionals ("if . . . then"), and the like. Basic connective concepts are not new to us. Our familiarity with them goes back to when we were first learning our mother tongue. And given years of practice, we've become extremely skilled in employing them not only in their basic meanings but in their subtle variations and nuances as well.

Those variations and nuances add a richness to discourse. But they can also create difficulties. They can lead to misunderstandings and confusion. Of course, we often have disputes over substantive concepts like murder. But even familiar and seemingly innocent connectives can generate disagreements if we are not clear about what we mean by them. Indeed, even questions of life and death sometimes hang on simple connectives.

The Eighth Amendment of the US Constitution forbids certain sorts of punishments: "Excessive bail shall not be required, nor excessive fines imposed, nor cruel and unusual punishment inflicted." Not surprisingly, there are disputes over what in this context counts as "cruel" punishment and over what "unusual" might include. But there are also disagreements over the seemingly simple term *and*, not only in the courts but even in Andrea's dorm room. Is Andrea right that it means that cruel punishment is forbidden *and, moreover,* that unusual punishment is forbidden as well? If so, then any punishment that is *either* cruel *or* unusual is constitutionally forbidden, as Andrea maintained. Or is René right that it means to forbid only those punishments that are simultaneously *both* cruel *and* unusual? If so, even if capital punishment is taken to be cruel, it is not constitutionally forbidden since it's not unusual. Which is it? Whether the death penalty is constitutionally permitted may depend upon the answer to this question.

Other connectives can also generate ambiguities. The disjunction "or" can be employed in more than one way. For instance, the official Mega Millions Lottery website says that the winner has "the choice of a Cash Option or an Annual Payout." You would not get very far if you asked for both. Here, "or" is used in the *exclusive* sense and means roughly the following:

> *exactly* one of the two alternatives, *excluding* the possibility of both.

The winner gets to—and has to—choose only one. On the other hand, the federal controlled substances act (Title 21 US Code) forbids "Manufacture or distribution of controlled substances for purposes of unlawful importation . . .". If you got in trouble with the law on this point, it would do you little good to claim that you had, after all, both manufactured and distributed controlled substances, thus escaping the "or" statement in that law. In this case, "or" is used in the *inclusive* sense, meaning, roughly,

> *at least* one of the two alternatives, *including* the possibility of both.

As we'll see in a later chapter, even negation can get a bit tricky. If someone is *not un*athletic, does that mean that she really *is* athletic? And as we'll see in the chapter on counterfactuals, the conditional connective ("if . . . then") is not as straightforward as it seems.

II. Truth Tables

In contexts where precision is essential—such as technical philosophical discussions, argument evaluation, laws, verdicts, constitutions, contracts, and international treaties—we need to clarify and nail down meanings as exactly as we can in order to forestall misunderstanding and confusion. One way of doing that in logic is to define logical connectives in terms of **truth tables**.

Connectives typically link two or more propositions to make a **compound proposition**. Every proposition has a truth-value; it is either true or false but cannot be both at the same time. Consider a conjunction:

> 1. (*P* and *Q*)

(where the letters *P* and *Q* each represent propositions). Proposition 1 is a compound proposition, containing two constituent propositions (called **conjuncts**). Each of those constituent conjuncts has its own truth-value. Each is either true or false. But the compound proposition itself will also have a single overall truth-value. How is the overall truth-value of the conjunction determined?

All of the basic connectives in logic are **truth-functional**. The overall truth or falsity of a compound proposition formed by a specific connective is determined just by the truth-values of the simpler constituent propositions involved as related by that specific connective. A conjunction such as proposition 1 above nearly always means that *both* constituent propositions (*P*, *Q*) are true. So if in proposition 1 one of the two constituent propositions turned out to be false, we would think that proposition 1 was not completely true. Proposition 1 asserted the truth of two things. But it got at least one of those two things wrong. So it's wrong overall. That sort of intuitive thinking underlies the basic truth tables for most connectives.

Logicians employ truth tables as a way of making the meanings of the various connectives absolutely clear and unambiguous in the context of logic. A truth table is a bit like a spreadsheet for truth-values. The basic idea is this: we lay out every possible combination of truth and falsehood for each of the constituent propositions of a compound proposition in a table of possible truth-values. Then for each such combination of possible truth-values, the resulting truth-value for the compound proposition is specified in the truth table. Again, since the connectives are truth-functional, the overall truth-value of the compound proposition itself will be determined exclusively by the truth-values of the constituent propositions plus the type of connective involved. This may sound complicated. But as with so many things in logic, the underlying idea is entirely familiar. A couple of examples should make this clear.

IIA. TRUTH TABLE FOR CONJUNCTION: $P \wedge Q$

We'll start with the truth table for conjunction. In truth tables we use capital letters such as P, Q, and R to represent various propositions, just as we did in the chapter on deduction. This not only saves us a ton of work writing out entire propositions every time, but it also allows us to see underlying logical structures more easily. In the truth table below, the letters P and Q represent any two propositions, and **T** and **F** represent the truth-values *true* and *false* respectively. The various truth-value possibilities are laid out schematically as follows:

P	Q	$P \wedge Q$
T	T	T
T	F	F
F	T	F
F	F	F

Here's how to read the truth table. Going from left to right, the top line says that where P is true and Q is true, their conjunction $(P \wedge Q)$ is also true. A conjunction says that both of its constituent propositions are true, and when that is correct, the conjunction itself is true as well. The second line says that where P is true but Q is false, the conjunction itself is false. In this case, the conjunction says that both its constituents are true, but it doesn't get it right: one of the constituents (Q) is false. So the conjunction itself is mistaken. Even though one of its constituents was true, the other wasn't. The third and fourth lines on the truth table follow the same pattern.

Note that every possible combination of **T** and **F** for the component propositions P and Q is represented on the truth table. In every possible case, the truth or falsity of the compound conjunction $P \wedge Q$ itself depends only on the truth-values of the component propositions. That means that the connective for the conjunction is truth-functional. You will note that the above truth table has four lines. In general, a truth table involving n constituent propositions will require 2^n lines. Thus, to represent every possible combination of truth-values for two propositions, 2^2 (= 4) lines will be required. A truth table involving three propositions will require 2^3 (= 8) lines. And so on. Truth tables can get out of hand pretty quickly. A truth table involving 10 constituent propositions would require 2^{10} lines. That's more than 1,000 lines.

Most of the other truth tables for basic connectives follow a straightforward and intuitive pattern. But there are a couple connectives where we have to make decisions about what we mean. Recall the two senses of the disjunction "or," the inclusive sense and the exclusive sense. Below are their respective truth tables.

IIB. TRUTH TABLE FOR INCLUSIVE DISJUNCTION: $P \vee Q$ (AT LEAST ONE, POSSIBLY BOTH)

P	Q	$P \vee Q$
T	T	T
T	F	T
F	T	T
F	F	F

Note that here again, as with all truth tables, each possible combination of truth and falsehood for the constituent propositions (P, Q) is represented on a separate line of the truth table. This truth table says that the inclusive disjunction is true whenever either or both of its constituents are true. It only takes one true constituent proposition to make $P \vee Q$ true, but if both are true that's covered too: manufacture or distribution of controlled substances, *or both*. As we'll see in a moment, the truth table for the exclusive sense is different, since its meaning is different.

IIc. TRUTH TABLE FOR EXCLUSIVE DISJUNCTION: $P \veebar Q$ (EXACTLY ONE, NOT BOTH)

P	Q	$P \veebar Q$
T	T	F
T	F	T
F	T	T
F	F	F

This truth table says that the exclusive disjunction itself is true whenever exactly one of its constituents is true. But the case where both are true is ruled out: either a lump-sum payout or an annual payment, but *no way do you get both*. The key difference is reflected in the first line of the two truth tables.

Just so everyone is on the same page, in logic we take the *inclusive* sense as the default value for disjunction. In cases where the exclusive sense is clearly meant or is the obviously appropriate sense, an additional adjustment is made. Be that as it may, the argument form of disjunctive syllogism that you learned earlier is valid for both senses of "or."

Having laid out the truth tables for conjunctions and disjunctions we can now add this note. In representing the logical structure of a compound statement that uses more than one connective, we sometimes need to insert parentheses to indicate which parts of the statement belong together. This too is a matter of removing ambiguity. Consider the following mathematical formula: $7 + 10 \times 3 = x$. If we added 7 and 10 together first and then multiplied by 3, x would equal 51. But if we added 7 to the product of 10 and 3, x would equal 37. That's quite a difference in the value of x. But without the use of parentheses, it's not clear what the value of x should be. We can remove the ambiguity by adding parentheses according to our intent, for instance: $7 + (10 \times 3) = x$. So, $x = 37$. Likewise in logic, the statement $P \vee R \wedge Q$ is ambiguous: it could indicate $(P \vee R) \wedge Q$ or $P \vee (R \wedge Q)$. On the first way of taking it, if P and R are true but Q is false, the compound statement is false; but on the second way of taking it, the compound statement is true. So we need to make the groupings of the simple statements clear through the use of parentheses.

IID. TRUTH TABLE FOR NEGATION: ~P

P	~P
T	F
F	T

The truth table for negation is straightforward and intuitive: if proposition P is in fact true, then the negation of P has to be false. To *deny* something that is actually true is to get on the wrong side of truth. That basic idea, embodied in the first line of the truth table for negation, goes back at least to Aristotle's *Metaphysics*, where Aristotle speaks of negation in these terms: "To say of what is that it is not, or of what is not that it is, is false" (*Metaphysics*, 1011b 25).

On the flip side, if proposition P is in fact false, then to say that P is false is to get it exactly right. And that is what the second line tells us. Note that since there is only one proposition involved, P, the number of truth table lines required will be 2^1 (= 2). Since there is only one constituent proposition, negation is sometimes referred to as a unary connective.

IIE. TRUTH TABLE FOR CONDITIONAL: $P \rightarrow Q$

P	Q	$P \rightarrow Q$
T	T	T
T	F	F
F	T	T
F	F	T

The conditional defined by this truth table is called a **material conditional**. The truth table for the material conditional $P \rightarrow Q$ requires a bit of explanation. Indeed, it threatens to derail some of our ordinary intuitions. But not to worry—we'll get them back on track later.

The second line on the conditional truth table is unproblematic. The proposition $P \rightarrow Q$ asserts that *if* P is true, *then* Q will be too. Suppose that P is in fact true, but that Q remains stubbornly false. In that situation, it is obvious that the conditional has just plain gotten things wrong. It is clearly false. Thus the second line on the truth table is exactly as we would anticipate: if the antecedent P is true and the consequent Q is false, then the conditional $P \rightarrow Q$ is itself false.

The first line may seem plausible as well. Suppose that we are evaluating the compound proposition that if P is true then Q is true too. It turns out that P is in fact true, so we check Q and, sure enough, it is true too. So hasn't the conditional then gotten things right? Well, in some cases, perhaps. But other cases seem less plausible. For a material conditional, there are no restrictions on what propositions P and Q can represent. They need not have any special connection to each other. Indeed, they can be utterly irrelevant to each other. All that counts is their individual truth-values. That means that according to the truth table for material conditional ($P \rightarrow Q$), the following propositions are all *true*:

- If John Kennedy had children, then Jupiter is the largest planet in our solar system.
- If Socrates was Greek, then some fast foods contain artificial ingredients.
- If some bankers are wealthy, then many people have watched lunar eclipses.
- If pink is some children's favorite color of socks, then some famous early Americans liked beer.

Something is weird here. If someone ever *seriously* said any of those things to you, insisting that you agree to their obvious truth, you would back slowly away from them, saying reassuring things in a soothing voice until you got far enough away to turn and run like crazy. Yet, the truth table solemnly declares these statements to be true.

And it gets worse. Notice that according to the last two lines of the truth table, any material conditional that has just any old false proposition whatever as an antecedent is thereby automatically a true conditional, no matter what the consequent is, no matter whether there is some connection between antecedent and consequent, no matter whether the consequent is true or false. Thus, the truth table for the material conditional declares the following to be indisputable truths:

- If the posted speed limit in most residential areas is 26 mph [it's actually 25 mph], then the novel *War and Peace* was written by a very clever cucumber.
- If you had earned one more penny last summer, then the moon would have instantly ceased to exist.

- If the book *The Singing Life of Birds—An Intimate Guide to the Private Lives of Birds: How, When, Why and Where Birds Sing* has 481 pages [it actually has 482 pages], then next month Martian alien invaders will appoint you as dictator of the world for life.

Those conditionals statements seem like utter nonsense. But the truth table says they are true. Can't logicians do any better than this?

Actually there is a very good reason for this strangeness. Here the truth table is *not* an attempt to capture what we mean in ordinary conversation when we say "if . . . then." Nor is it an attempt to define conditions for the truth or falsehood of many ordinary "if . . . then" statements. One part of those tasks emerges in the chapter on counterfactuals, another part in the chapter on modal logic. The truth table for the material conditional shown above is intended primarily as a tool for the evaluation of the validity of a specific class of deductive arguments. And despite the fact that it would *not* be a good tool for capturing meanings of ordinary conditionals, as a tool for the evaluation of the validity of arguments it works very well. In a wide array of deductive arguments, treating conditionals as material conditionals allows us to accurately determine whether the logic of those arguments is deductively correct. We will discuss the application of truth tables to whole arguments shortly.

III. Truth Tables and Tautologies

We commonly use the term **tautology** to refer to any statement that is in some sense internally redundant, circular, or in some similar way trivially true. For instance, a popular slogan among opponents of gun control is "If guns are outlawed, then only outlaws will have guns."

This statement is trivially true because if guns are outlawed, then anyone with a gun will be *by that very fact* in violation of the law. The same is true of bubble gum: if bubble gum were outlawed, then only outlaws will have bubble gum. Gun-control opponents probably intend to say something more substantial, something like: if guns are outlawed, then the *only* people with guns will be those who are *already* outlaws for some *other* reason. That, of course, seems plainly false. Members of the police force would still have guns; so would members of the military. Gun-control opponents may have a sensible point in mind, but they have not quite captured it in that slogan.

In logic, "tautology" refers to a specific type of *necessary truth*. A proposition P is necessarily true if it is logically impossible for it to be false—if there is no way, under any real, imaginable, or remotely possible circumstance that P is, can be, or ever could have been false. This concept will be discussed in much more detail in the chapter on modal logic. For present purposes, we can say that a tautology is a compound proposition that turns out true on every line of its truth table. Recall that truth tables are constructed so that they contain every possible combination of truth-values for the component propositions.

Let's consider some simple cases to see how this works. First, the statement "If P is true, then P is true" is clearly a tautology form. Clearly, that sort of conditional has to be true no matter what P is. Here's the truth table for this statement:

P	$P \to P$
T	T
F	T

In this case, the antecedent and consequent are the same proposition: P. On the first line, since P is true, then both antecedent and consequent are true. If we look back to the truth table for conditionals, we see that if both antecedent and consequent are true, then the conditional itself is true. On the second line, since P is false, both antecedent and consequent are false. If we again look back to the truth table for conditionals, we see that if both antecedent and consequent are false, then the conditional itself is true. So every line on the truth table for $P \to P$ is true. And since P can only be either true or false (never both at the same time), every possible combination of truth-values for antecedent and consequent is represented on the two lines of truth table. It is thus not possible for $P \to P$ to ever, under any possible circumstances, be false. Hence it is a tautology.

Here's a second case. Consider the proposition "either P is true or P is false" ($P \lor \sim P$). It seems obvious that this statement is a tautology. And we can demonstrate that it is indeed a tautology by way of a truth table. There is only one component proposition, P, and it can be only true or false. We list those possibilities in the first column. But the negation of P (that is, $\sim P$) also factors into the overall compound proposition as one of its disjuncts. So it will make things a bit easier if we display the truth-values of each part of the final proposition as a preliminary step as well. We know from the truth table for negation that whenever P is true, ~*P* will be false, and that whenever *P* is false, ~*P* will be true. Thus:

P	~*P*	*P* ∨ ~*P*
T	F	
F	T	

Now only the final step remains. On the first line, where *P* is true, the disjunction *P* ∨ ~*P* contains one true disjunct (the left-hand one) and one false disjunct (the right-hand one). According to the truth table for disjunction that makes *P* ∨ ~*P* true. On the second line, where *P* is false, the disjunction *P* ∨ ~*P* contains one false disjunct (the left-hand one) and one true disjunct (the right hand one). According to the truth table for disjunction that again makes *P* ∨ ~*P* true. Filling in the remaining spots accordingly, we end up with

P	~*P*	*P* ∨ ~*P*
T	F	T
F	T	T

Here again, every possible truth-value of the component propositions is represented, and every line on the truth table under the proposition *P* ∨ ~*P* is true. Thus, the proposition *P* ∨ ~*P* is also a tautology. Note that in this case it does not matter which sense of "or" is involved, exclusive or inclusive. Either way, *P* ∨ ~*P* still comes out as a tautology. Remember, however, that unless otherwise indicated in or by the context, the inclusive sense is taken as the default.

Let's do one more slightly more complicated example. Take the proposition "If (*P* and *Q*) is true, then *Q* is true." This is expressed symbolically as (*P* ∧ *Q*) → *Q*. To see that this statement is a tautology, we construct its truth table. Since the compound proposition *P* ∧ *Q* is the antecedent of the proposition under consideration, we'll give it its own column.

P	*Q*	*P* ∧ *Q*	(*P* ∧ *Q*) → *Q*
T	T	T	
T	F	F	
F	T	F	
F	F	F	

We now fill in the truth-values of $(P \land Q) \rightarrow Q$:

P	Q	$P \land Q$	$(P \land Q) \rightarrow Q$
T	T	T	T
T	F	F	T
F	T	F	T
F	F	F	T

Notice that every row under $(P \land Q) \rightarrow Q$ is assigned **T**. The conjunction $P \land Q$, which forms the antecedent of the conditional statement, is true only in row 1, where P is true and Q is true. But rows 2, 3, and 4 follow the peculiar logic of the material conditional, where, if the antecedent is false, the conditional as a whole is true. And so, on every possible combination of the truth-values of its constituent simple statements, $(P \land Q) \rightarrow Q$ comes out true. This is the mark of a tautology.

What does the truth table look like if something is not a tautology? There will be at least one possible circumstance in which the proposition in question can be false (i.e., the truth table will have at least one line on which the proposition in question does not come out true).

Let's test this proposition: $P \rightarrow (P \rightarrow Q)$. We begin by setting up the truth table with all possible combination of truth-values for P and Q, and with a column for the subcomponent $P \rightarrow Q$:

P	Q	$P \rightarrow Q$	$P \rightarrow (P \rightarrow Q)$
T	T	T	
T	F	F	
F	T	T	
F	F	T	

Filling in the column for the overall proposition $P \rightarrow (P \rightarrow Q)$ we get

P	Q	$P \rightarrow Q$	$P \rightarrow (P \rightarrow Q)$
T	T	T	T
T	F	F	F
F	T	T	T
F	F	T	T

As the truth table shows, $P \to (P \to Q)$ is not a tautology. When P is true and Q is false, the entire proposition is false.

IV. Truth Tables and Logical Equivalence

One other important logical factor can be exhibited in truth tables. Notice that in the last truth table, the truth values for the proposition $P \to Q$ and the truth-values for $P \to (P \to Q)$ are absolutely identical on every line. No matter what the truth-values of P and Q, $P \to Q$ and $P \to (P \to Q)$ will either both be true, or both be false. Any two (or more) propositions that can never differ in truth-value, which are always either true or false together, are **logically equivalent**. This equivalence is symbolized by a "triple bar" ($\equiv$). Thus,

$$(P \to Q) \equiv [P \to (P \to Q)]$$

Obviously, any proposition is logically equivalent to itself:

$$P \equiv P$$

There are zillions of logical equivalences, and you can only hope that your philosophy instructor will not make you learn them all. But there are a number of logical equivalences that play important roles in logic, and some have even been given names. Following are just a few of those key logical equivalences:

Double negation:	$P \equiv \sim\sim P$
Identity:	$(P \land P) \equiv P$
	$(P \lor P) \equiv P$
Contraposition:	$(P \to Q) \equiv (\sim Q \to \sim P)$
De Morgan's Laws:	$\sim(P \land Q) \equiv (\sim P \lor \sim Q)$
	$\sim(P \lor Q) \equiv (\sim P \land \sim Q)$

To get a sense for the logical equivalences captured in these statements, it might be helpful to read them out. For instance, the first of De Morgan's Laws says that it is not the case that both P and Q are true if and only if either P is false or Q is false.

V. Truth Tables and Contradictions

We might think of a **contradiction** as part of the dark side of logic. It is a proposition that is as far from the unfailing truth of tautologies as it can possibly get. Whereas a tautology is true for every possible situation and every possible combination of truth-values for its constituent propositions, a contradiction is false for every possible situation and in every possible combination of truth-values for its constituent propositions. For instance, suppose that you are listening to a political debate and one candidate says:

2. It is indeed true that global warming is occurring right now.

Shortly thereafter the other candidate says:

3. It simply is not true that global warming is occurring right now.

Obviously there is no way that both of these statements can be true at the same time. They contradict each other. Worse yet, if the same candidate says *both* (2) *and* (3), then that candidate has made contradictory claims. The candidate has engaged in a self-contradiction. There are various subtypes of contradictions, but the basic underlying character of any contradiction is to *both affirm and deny exactly the same thing*. All contradictions, then, reduce to this basic propositional form:

$P \wedge {\sim} P$

Here the *same* proposition (P) is being simultaneously affirmed and denied. Intuitively, a contradiction is any statement that is in some sense logically inconsistent with itself and thus necessarily false. A historically influential definition characterizes contradictions this way:

To say that a pair of propositions is *contradictory* means:
a. it is logically impossible for both to be simultaneously true, and
b. it is logically impossible for both to be simultaneously false.

Sometimes it is said that a contradiction involves claiming that some thing both does and does not have some particular property, for instance,

R. John is a married bachelor.

But *not* being married is part of the very concept *bachelor*, so R is actually saying that it is true that *John is married*, and simultaneously that it is false that *John is married*. As you can see, that's a repeat of the same basic form of contradiction displayed above. Some philosophers also use the term "contradiction" in an extended sense to refer to any proposition that is *necessarily false*. Be that as it may, we can safely say that all contradictions are necessary falsehoods just as all tautologies are necessary truths. **Contingent propositions** are propositions that are neither tautologies nor contradictions. They may be true or false. We will have more to say about these matters in the chapter on modal logic.

Let's look at the truth table for the general contradiction form: $P \wedge \sim P$. We begin with all possible combinations of truth-values for P. Since the compound proposition involves the conjunction of two propositions (P, $\sim P$) we can add in a column for $\sim P$ just to keep our accounting clear. The basic truth table for negation gives us the appropriate truth values for $\sim P$:

P	$\sim P$	$P \wedge \sim P$
T	F	
F	T	

We now consult the truth table for conjunction, one conjunct here being P, the other $\sim P$. Since any conjunction of a true proposition and a false proposition is false, the truth values for the overall proposition will be

P	$\sim P$	$P \wedge \sim P$
T	F	F
F	T	F

As indicated, the conjunction $P \wedge \sim P$ is false no matter what the truth-value of P. So that conjunction is a contradiction.

We can now also see the sense in which tautologies and contradictions are on opposite sides of the truth. Let's look at the truth table for the negation of the contradiction $P \wedge \sim P$. We can add a new column to the truth table just above:

P	~P	P ∧ ~P	~(P ∧ ~P)
T	F	F	
F	T	F	

Whenever the compound proposition $P \wedge \sim P$ is false, its negation $\sim(P \wedge \sim P)$ is true. And since $P \wedge \sim P$ is always false, $\sim(P \wedge \sim P)$ is always true (i.e., it is a tautology):

P	~P	P ∧ ~P	~(P ∧ ~P)
T	F	F	T
F	T	F	T

That is a universal pattern. Every negation of a contradiction is a tautology. Likewise, every negation of a tautology is a contradiction.

Two more quick notes. First, the impossibility of contradictions ever being true has been encapsulated in various versions of the **law of noncontradiction** at least since the time of Aristotle. Aristotle gave several different versions, but here is perhaps the most prominent one:

> **Law of Noncontradiction:** It is impossible for the same thing to belong and not to belong at the same time to the same thing and in the same respect. (Aristotle, *Metaphysics* 1005b 19)

Second, Aristotle (and many others) have held that the law of noncontradiction is a fundamental presupposition of all rational thought, and that without that assumption there could not even be any knowledge. Indeed Aristotle believed that contradictions are *unthinkable*—not in the sense that a contradiction would be really unfortunate or disastrous, but that we literally cannot think contradictions, we simply cannot even remotely imagine what it would be like for a contradiction to be true. It would of course follow that it is not possible for someone to actually believe contradictory propositions.

VI. Truth Tables, Tautologies, and Validity

Truth tables can also be employed to determine the validity or invalidity of some (but not all) types of deductive arguments. Remember the definition of validity: an argument is deductively valid just in case it is *necessarily true* that *if* all the premises of the argument are true, *then* the conclusion of the argument will be true as well. That definition contains a conditional ("if . . . then") in which the antecedent involves the argument's premises and the consequent involves the argument's conclusion. Thus, an argument is deductively valid if the conditional corresponding to the argument is a tautology. In other words, an argument is deductively valid when the corresponding conditional,

If (all the premises are true) *then* (the conclusion is true)

is a tautology.

As an example, recall that the form for modus ponens involves two premises and a conclusion:

$P \rightarrow Q$
P
Therefore,
Q

We now form the corresponding conditional:

If ($P \rightarrow Q$ and P are both true) *then* (Q is true as well)
that is, $[(P \rightarrow Q) \wedge P] \rightarrow Q$
(the square brackets "[" and "]" work just like parentheses)

We can verify that this conditional is a tautology via its truth table:

P	Q	$P \rightarrow Q$	P	$(P \rightarrow Q) \wedge P$	Q	$[(P \rightarrow Q) \wedge P] \rightarrow Q$
		first premise	*second premise*	*antecedent*	*consequent/ conclusion*	*entire conditional*
T	T	T	T	T	T	T
T	F	F	T	F	F	T
F	T	T	F	F	T	T
F	F	T	F	F	F	T

There is thus no possible circumstance, no possible combination of truth-values, under which both the premises $P \rightarrow Q$ and P could be true but the conclusion *Q* would be false. That confirms for us that the modus ponens form does indeed meet the requirement for deductive validity.

Summary and Conclusion

For any compound proposition, a truth table displays the truth-values of that proposition for every possible combination of the truth-values of its constituent propositions taken together with their logical connectives. Truth tables are useful for a variety of purposes. They can make clear the exact meaning of the logical connectives we employ in the discipline of logic. They can also be used to assess the validity of many deductive arguments. But as you can imagine, truth tables for very complicated arguments with lots of premises can get extremely messy, not to mention tedious. An argument containing seven constituent propositions would require a truth table with 128 lines. It is in part for that reason that more powerful and efficient methods for assessing validity involving structured types of derivation and deduction processes have been developed. But those are beyond the scope of this text.

3.

Quantification

There are many deductive arguments that cannot be evaluated using just the concepts and techniques discussed in the first chapter. One set of additional techniques involves quantification. Suppose that the initial dispute between Andrea and René about the soul has moved on to the possibility of an afterlife. Andrea is characteristically skeptical:

> You have to admit that scientific studies have shown that all thought and awareness depend directly upon electro-chemical activity in the brain. That means no electrochemical brain activity, no mental activity. And after death, there is no electrochemical brain activity. Everybody knows *that*. So, since Napoleon is dead, he cannot be aware of anything right now. Obviously, then, there is no life after death, for Napoleon or anyone else.

I. Quantification: The Basic Concept

In her argument against belief in the afterlife, Andrea proposed some general principles ("*all* thought," "*no* electrochemical brain activity") and applied those principles to a very specific case: Napoleon. Then she used that application as the basis for a general conclusion ("*no* life after death"). Those moves involve more than just deductive inferences between whole propositions. They involve what logicians call **quantifiers**— concepts such as "all", "some", "none," and the like; quantifiers address the internal logical structure of simple propositions and represent their scope. As such, they are the stock-in-trade of what is known as **predicate logic**.

"All," "none," and similar terms that assert something universal are termed *universal quantifiers*. Thus, "*All* kittens are fuzzy" and "*No* alligators are fuzzy" are universally quantified statements. "Some" and similar terms that assert the actual existence of one or more things in specific categories are termed *existential quantifiers*. Thus, "*Some* kittens have no tails" and "*At least one* book was stolen" are existentially quantified statements.

II. Quantification: Some Basic Principles

Although we could get into some technical complexities if we went very deep into quantifiers, there are some straightforward basic principles that we can introduce here. Here is just one example. We can easily see that if something is universally true of everything, if it applies to absolutely everything, then it must apply to any particular thing we wish to think about. Here's an example of how that principle works:

> Since everything physical was created by God,
> it follows that the apple in your lunch was created by God.

That very simple principle is what logicians call universal instantiation. It takes something that is true of everything and applies it in a specific instance.

> **Universal Instantiation (UI)**
>   1. Everything has property *P*.
> Therefore,
>   2. This specific thing (whatever it is) has property *P*.

So, as Andrea argues,

> Everything that lacks electrochemical brain activity has no awareness.
> Therefore,
> Napoleon, lacking electrochemical brain activity, has no awareness.

Going in the reverse direction—from specific cases to universal statements—is much trickier. In fact, going from specific to general often involves the fallacy of hasty generalization, discussed in the chapter on informal fallacies in this text. But under certain narrowly specified conditions, deductively valid generalizations from specific instances is possible. In fact, we saw an instance of that in Andrea's argument about life after death. When Andrea wanted an example of a case where there was no electrochemical brain activity, she picked Napoleon at random. The case she was making did not involve anything we know about Napoleon that is not also true of any other person she could have picked as an example: George Washington, Attila the Hun, Mary Queen of Scots, Mussolini, Jimi Hendrix, Christa McAuliffe, or absolutely anyone else no longer living. Had she applied to everyone something that applied to Napoleon but not, so far as she knew, to everyone else—like being in love with Josephine—that would have been a serious mistake.

Andrea argues that Napoleon, now lacking any electrochemical brain activity and thus having no awareness, is not continuing to live after death. But she could have logically concluded exactly the same thing about *everyone* no longer living on exactly the same grounds she appealed to concerning Napoleon's extinction. And since a conclusion concerning *everyone* no longer living is a universally quantified statement, Andrea's inference from Napoleon to *every* such instance is deductively correct. Of course, that doesn't mean that her conclusion is correct. There might be other problems in her argument (e.g., false premises). But given her premises, her inference was legitimate. That sort of inference is called universal generalization.

Universal Generalization (UG)
Specific instance *x* has property *P*.
[*Condition: all of our grounds for thinking that x has property P apply equally to any and every other instance we might have chosen.*]
Therefore,
Every instance has property *P*.

Often the difficult part of UG is establishing the condition for specific arguments. And specifying all the technicalities of the condition can get complicated. But the above is the rough idea.

Much less logically demanding are inferences to existentially quantified conclusions. If we know of a *specific* entity that some principle or property applies to, we can conclude that there is at least one thing in the category in question. So, for instance, if your copy of Kant's *Critique of Pure Reason* tragically fell out of your book bag and was lost, it follows that there is at least one thing that fell out of your book bag and was lost.

That very intuitive principle is referred to as existential generalization.

> **Existential Generalization (EG)**
>
> This specific thing has property *P*.
>
> Therefore,
>
> There exists at least one thing that has property *P*.

There is, however, one more tricky inference in arguments involving quantification. As viewers of prime-time law enforcement dramas are aware, detectives often know that some specific crime, say, a bank robbery, was committed by *someone*, but they don't know the identity of the criminal. Fortunately, they generally find out right before the final commercial. During the investigation, they need to be able to discuss what they know about the unknown perpetrator. But until they discover the criminal's identity, they must refer to the person without having the real name. It gets a bit awkward always having to say, "The as-yet-unidentified perpetrator of this bank robbery, whoever he or she may turn out to be, must be 5'10" tall and left-handed." In order to simplify reference, detectives will sometimes pick a fake name at random: "Jane Doe is the bank robber" and "Jane Doe must be 5'10" tall and left-handed."

Having a name chosen just for convenience in discussion also makes drawing inferences about the unknown criminal less awkward. For instance,

> "Jane Doe" is left-handed.
>
> Most left-handed people write with a distinctive slant.
>
> Therefore,
>
> "Jane Doe" probably writes with a distinctive slant as well.

But the detectives have to be careful here. Suppose that a rookie detective thinking, "Jane Doe is the bank robber," decides to google "Jane Doe" and finds that strangely enough there is a woman actually named Jane Doe living in the city. The rookie tracks her down, hauls her into the station, and charges her with bank robbery. Obviously, the rookie has made a serious mistake. The detectives were using the name Jane Doe as a purely made-up name (or so everyone else thought) for convenience in discussion. To take that to be an *actual* name, and to pin the crime on some person who happens to have that name is to completely misunderstand the situation. In fact, suppose that the detectives had just happened to choose "Melissa"? Or worse, what if they had come up with *your* name by some wild coincidence? Arresting you on that basis would be a serious mistake. At least, we'll *hope* you weren't by coincidence the actual perpetrator. Melissa? Well, who knows?

Again, it often simplifies discussion, inferences, arguments and the like, to have a name for something instead of a complicated description. But the crucial point is this: we cannot use the coincidence of that name *already* applying to something else (e.g., the actual Jane Doe) to draw further conclusions (e.g., that the actual Jane Doe is the bank robber).

Temporarily assigning an artificial name for ease of reference is called existential instantiation, and as the above indicates, we must use it with care.

> **Existential instantiation (EI)**
>   1. Some unknown thing or other has property P.
> Therefore,
>   2. α (a made-up, temporary, fake name) has property P.
>   [*Condition: if there is something that already has the name α, we cannot apply anything we know specifically about either of the α's to the other one.*]

As with the special condition in universal generalization, getting the precise details of the condition right in many of its applications often is difficult. But the above is the rough idea.

We can now add a couple more items to our catalog of symbols. In representing the internal logical structure of a simple proposition, we can use a lowercase x as a variable ranging over individual things, and a capital P to stand for some property of a thing. If we wanted to show the structure of a statement in which we predicate a property of something, we would write the property symbol first, followed by the individual variable: Px. This would stand for the general form of a statement, like "Arnold is priceless." The statement that something P is true of everything—that everything is P—is symbolized as

$(x)Px$ (sometimes you may also see "$(\forall x)Px$")

Here the x in parentheses, (x), is called the *universal quantifier*. It is to be read, "For all x . . ."

The statement that some thing(s) are P is symbolized as

$(\exists x)Px$

$(\exists x)$ is the symbol called the *existential quantifier*. It is to be read, "There is some x . . ." or "There is at least one x . . ."

As it turns out, existential and universal quantifiers are closely related in some intuitive ways. For instance, saying that *everything* has some characteristic P is exactly the same as saying that there isn't anything that does not have that characteristic. So,

$(x)Px$

and

$\sim(\exists x)\sim Px$

are just two different ways of saying the same thing—or, as logicians say, those two are **logically equivalent**. Logical equivalence can be symbolized by the triple bar ($\equiv$), the biconditional connective that means "if and only if." It's implication going both ways. So we can write the above equivalence this way:

$(x)Px \equiv \sim(\exists x)\sim Px$

Similarly, saying, "At least one thing has some characteristic P," is exactly the same as saying, "It is not true that absolutely everything lacks characteristic P." Thus,

$(\exists x)Px$

and

$\sim(x)\sim Px$

are logically equivalent as well. Symbolically, this is expressed as

$(\exists x)Px \equiv \sim(x)\sim Px$

III. Quantifiers and Familiar Deductive Arguments

Quantifiers allow us to see into the forms of some arguments more clearly. Take the old standard philosophical example of an argument:

1. All humans are mortal.
2. Socrates is human.

Therefore,

3. Socrates is mortal.

To understand why this argument is deductively valid, we have to look into the scope of the simple statements involved. We recognize in the first premise a universal statement concerning all humans. It says of all humans that they are mortal. Logicians read that statement as a conditional: if something is a human, then that something is mortal. But we know from universal instantiation that if something is true of everything, it is true of any specific thing we want to talk about. So, from

1. All humans are mortal
   (i.e., if something is human, then it is mortal)

it follows that

1a. If Socrates is human then Socrates is mortal
    (from universal instantiation of premise 1).

And since

2. Socrates is human (the second premise of our argument).

It follows that

3. Socrates is mortal (by modus ponens using 1a and 2).

There are a number of other very complex principles involving universal and existential quantifiers, but we need not pursue those complexities here.

IV. Testing for Invalidity

The rules of quantification can help us tell when an argument involving quantification is valid. How can we tell when an argument involving quantification is invalid, that is, when the conclusion does not follow from the premises? There are technical ways of doing this, but in many cases we can construct analogous cases—cases where the logical form of the argument is the same as the original, but where the premises are true and the conclusion is obviously false. Consider this argument:

1. All conservatives support our Second Amendment rights.
2. Lydia supports of our Second Amendment rights.

So: 3. So Lydia must be a conservative.

Does the conclusion of this argument follow? Here's an analogous argument:

1. All alligators have lungs.
2. Lydia has lungs.

So: 3. So Lydia must be an alligator.

The premises of this argument are true while the conclusion is false. So it's invalid: the premises of an argument with this logical form could be true while the conclusion is false. Since the argument about Lydia's political persuasion has the same logical form, that argument is also invalid.

V. Summary and Conclusion

In the first chapter we introduced the idea and some of the terms of propositional logic. Propositional logic concerns the logical relations *between* propositions. In the second chapter we introduced a method for clarifying the meaning of the various connectives we use to join simple propositions together to make compound propositions. In this chapter, on quantification, we have dealt with predicate logic, which brings into consideration the logical relations *within* simple propositions. Quantification concerns the scope of the predicate of a simple statement with respect to its subject (the predicate covers all, none, or some). In turn, the internal logic of propositions can give rise to certain valid forms of deductive inference between propositions, as we saw in the discussion of quantification rules.

There is much to both propositional logic and predicate logic that we have not covered. If you'd like to pursue these topics and acquire more sophisticated skills in the art of deduction, then a semester-long course in logic may be just the thing for you. In the next two chapters we will cover argument forms not often treated in introductory logic books.

These forms are, nonetheless, commonly used in everyday reasoning. They are not the exclusive property of philosophy majors or professional logicians. And so they have a place in a basic text that deals with the common ways in which we reason together with others in the search for what it true.

4.

Modal Logic

"WHAT!!?" shrieked René, turning around so abruptly she slopped coffee onto her sweatshirt.

"It's true," said Andrea. "Jeremy and David drove to Iowa Thursday and got married."

"But . . . they . . . it's not . . . they aren't . . .. They can't have," René spluttered.

"Well, they obviously *can* have, because they *did*. In fact, Melissa went along as a witness."

"But it can't be a real marriage. I mean, you have to admit that strictly speaking that's impossible, because the very definition of marriage is that it is a union between one man and one woman. That means that it *has* to be one man and one woman or it can't be an actual marriage."

"Oh come on, René. Definitions are just words. Words are something we humans make up. We invented them and we can use them any way we want to. We can even change them. Pluto used to be defined as a planet, right? Not now. And whales used to be defined as fish, right? But not anymore. Anyway, since when do mere words dictate reality—like what is or isn't actually possible or true? There were things that were true and things that were impossible long before there were any humans around to invent words."

"But that's exactly what I mean. I'm talking about the *concept* of marriage. And we don't get to make concepts up any way we want to. Concepts involve unchangeable truths—maybe they exist eternally in the mind of God. That would mean that they existed forever, long before humans invented anything. And real concepts *do* dictate what's true. And what's possible. And that means that Jeremy and David can't possibly be really, truly married—any more than a real circle can have four straight sides. It wouldn't be a circle, and this 'marriage' isn't a marriage."

As you can imagine, the discussion of gay marriage did not stop there. And of course it will get even livelier once Melissa gets back.

I. Modal Logic: Basic Concepts

Andrea and René's disagreement is not just about what *is* true or false—it's about what *can* or *can't* in principle be true, about what *must* be true or *must* be false. That's why their discussion is peppered with terms such as "can," "can't," "possible," "impossible," "may be," "has to be," and the like. Their disagreement is about *possibility* and *necessity*.

The area of logic that deals with possibility and necessity is called **modal logic**. The type of possibility and necessity modal logic addresses is **logical possibility** and **logical necessity**. Logical possibility and logical necessity are often different from what we mean when we talk about what's possible and what's necessary in everyday terms. Intuitively, we can think of basic modal ideas in logic this way:

Statement "*P* is *necessary*" (or "*P* is *necessarily true*") means roughly: it is logically impossible for *P* to be false. No matter what reality is like, no matter how different reality might have been, *P* is and would have been true. There is no way *P* could ever under any circumstances, real or imaginary, be false. (Note that "necessary," in the logical sense, does not mean anything like the everyday sense of necessary as "required," "important," or "essential.") Mathematical truths, conceptual truths, analytic truths, logical truths, tautologies, correct fundamental principles of metaphysics, and the like are typically considered to be necessarily true. Correct definitions are also often thought to embody **necessary truths**.

Statement "*P* is *impossible*" (or "*P* is *necessarily false*") means roughly: it is logically impossible for *P* to be true. No matter what reality is like, no matter how different reality might have been, *P* is and would have been false. There is no way *P* could ever under any circumstances, real or imaginary, be true. It does not just mean that *P* can't be true in current circumstances.

Logical contradictions, mathematical falsehoods, negations of necessary truths, and the like are typically considered to be necessarily false.

Statement "*P is possible*" (or "*P is possibly true*") means roughly: whether or not *P* is in fact true, there could be circumstances (perhaps very ordinary, perhaps very bizarre) in which *P* would be true—*P* is not in itself logically contradictory. It does not mean that *P* is possible given current circumstances.

Statement "*Not P is possible*" (or "*P is possibly false*") means roughly: whether or not *P* is in fact false, there could be (perhaps very ordinary, perhaps very bizarre) circumstances in which *P* would be false—*P* is not by itself logically necessary. It does not mean that *P* is impossible in current circumstances.

Statement "*P is contingent*" means roughly:
P is neither necessary nor impossible—it could be either true or false, depending upon circumstances.

That *P* is *contingently true* means that *P* is in fact true—it is true, but it did not necessarily have to be true; it could have been in fact false had things been different.

That *P* is *contingently false* means that *P* is in fact false—it is false, but it did not necessarily have to be false; it could have been in fact true had things been different.

You briefly met some of these concepts before in the chapter on deductive arguments. Recall the two versions of the definition of validity:

Valid$_1$: It is *not logically possible* for all the premises of the argument to be true and for the conclusion of the argument to be false at the same time.

Valid$_2$: It is *logically necessary* that if all the premises of the argument are true, then the conclusion of the argument is true as well.

The definition of validity is one key place where modal concepts function in philosophy. A few others will be discussed later.

II. Possible Worlds: A Conceptual Aid

Modal terms may seem a bit daunting. It can be difficult to keep modal ideas about necessity and possibility straight. But they are actually more straightforward than they might at first seem. One simple way of thinking about them was proposed by the German philosopher/mathematician G. W. Leibniz (1646–1716). Leibniz suggested that we imagine different ways God could have created the world, different ways things could have been. Some of those ways would have been very like our world—maybe just like it throughout its entire history and existence except for one difference: you were born at 8:03 a.m. instead of 8:02 a.m. Other worlds would be hugely different from ours. Some of them would contain no stars. In some of them there would be no humans. In some there might be humans, but they are destined to be destroyed in a vicious intergalactic war. In some of them you would never exist. In others you would be the imperial dictator of the entire solar system. And on and on. As you can see, there are infinitely many different ways that reality *could* have been. These different ways reality could have been Leibniz referred to as **possible worlds.** For some statement P to be true in a possible world just means that had that world been the real one, then P would have actually been true.

Of course we can't come close to imagining the entire range of possible worlds. But Leibniz suggested that we can think of necessary truths— things that logically could not fail to be true—as things that are true in all possible worlds. If some statement P logically *cannot* be false, then no matter how reality is constructed, P will be true. Thus

- *P is necessary* means *P is true in all possible worlds.*

Following this intuitive sort of reasoning we can also see that:

- *P is impossible* means *P is false in all possible worlds.*
- *P is possible* means *P is true in at least one possible world.*
- *P is contingent* means *P is true in some possible worlds, but is not true in others.*
- *P is in fact true* means *P is true in this possible world—the one actual world.*
- *P is in fact false* means *P is false in this possible world—the one actual world.*

III. Some Basic Modal Principles

The ideas of possibility and necessity are interrelated in a number of ways, and imagining possible worlds can make some of those ways easy to see. For instance, here are four basic modal principles, first stated in modal terms then rephrased in terms of possible worlds. When put into possible-worlds terms, the principles seem obviously true.

1. *If P is necessary, then P is true.*
   If *P* is true in *every* possible world, then *P* will be true in *this* possible world (the actual world).

2. *If P is true, then P is possible.*
   If *P* is true in *this* possible world, then there is *at least one* possible world in which *P* is true.

3. *If P is necessary, then it is impossible for P to be false.*
   If *P* is true in *every* possible world, then there will not be a single world in which it is *not* true.

4. *If P is possible, then P is not a necessary falsehood.*
   If there is *at least one* possible world in which *P* is true, then it is *not* true that *P* is false in every world.

IV. Modal Symbols

In the chapters on deductive arguments and quantification you were introduced to some logical symbols—several connectives and two quantifiers. We can now add two more symbols to the catalog, one for necessity and one for possibility:

P is necessary is symbolized as $\Box P$ (the symbol is called a *box*)
P is possible is symbolized as $\Diamond P$ (the symbol is called a *diamond*)

We can now symbolize the four principles given above:

1. *If P is necessary, then P is true*: $\Box P \rightarrow P$
2. *If P is true, then P is possible*: $P \rightarrow \Diamond P$
3. *If P is necessary, then it is not possible for P to be false*:
   $\Box P \rightarrow {\sim}\Diamond {\sim}P$

4. If P is possible, then P is not a necessary falsehood: $\Diamond P \to {\sim}\Box{\sim}P$

Principle 2 was employed by Andrea in the opening argument about gay marriage—it *did* happen, so it was clearly *possible.* René depended on principle 3: if necessarily marriage is between a man and a woman, then it is not possible for something not between a man and a woman to be a marriage.

Principles 3 and 4 work in the opposite direction as well. For instance, it is true that

If it is not possible for P to be false, then P is necessarily true:
${\sim}\Diamond{\sim}P \to \Box P$

However, principles 1 and 2 do not work in the reverse direction. For instance, the reverse of 2—that if *P* is *possible* then it is in fact *true*—is obviously mistaken.

V. Combining Symbols

We often combine modal symbols (or modal *operators,* as they are usually called) with the other symbols learned earlier. For instance, a conditional that is necessarily true is called a *logical entailment.* Here's a simple example:

If *number **n** is even,* then *number **n** is evenly divisible by 2.*

Let *E* represent *number **n** is even,* and *D* represent *number **n** is evenly divisible by 2;* we symbolize the conditional as follows:

$E \to D$

We show that this conditional is necessarily true—that it is an entailment—by putting a box in front of the entire conditional, which we enclose in parentheses:

$\Box(E \to D)$

We can build up even more complicated constructions by adding quantifiers. For instance, that it is necessarily true that everything has some characteristic C is symbolized as:

$$\Box(x)Cx$$

There are almost no limits to the degrees of complication possible by adding operators and other symbols together. There are also some conceptual disagreements over a small number of tricky modal formulas where several operators and symbols are put together. We won't go into those issues here. These disagreements have given rise to several slightly different modal logic systems, although there is general agreement on the fundamental modal formulas (including the basic principles above). The system accepted by most philosophers has the uninformative name S5. Here are a few examples of some of the principles of S5 that you can have fun thinking about in possible-worlds terms:

   i. $\Box P \to \Box\Box P$
   ii. $\Diamond\Box P \to \Box P$
   iii. $\Diamond P \to \Box\Diamond P$

Principle i is also true in the alternative system S4, although ii and iii are not. Principle ii states that if it is possible that P is necessarily true, then P is necessarily true. Principle iii states that if P is possible, then it is necessarily the case that P is possible. Try out your intuitions in possible-worlds talk and see what you think about these modal claims. Are you willing to go to S5, or would you rather stick with S4?

The existence of some conceptual disagreements is not something unique to modal logic. As we'll see in the chapter on probability, there are some deep conceptual disagreements among probability theorists. We find a similar situation among mathematicians over the legitimacy of some specific mathematical equations, over what constitutes a legitimate mathematical proof, and even over what numbers *are*.

VI. Some Extensions

The general structure of inferences and principles involving necessity and possibility turn out to have interesting applications in other conceptual areas as well. The primary areas have been epistemology (epistemic logic), ethics (deontic logic), issues involving time (temporal logic), and subjunctive or counterfactual logics (where possible-worlds ideas have been especially fruitful). Here are two brief examples, one from deontic logic and one from epistemic logic. First, epistemic logic.

Take the basic modal principle

$$\Box P \to P$$

As we've seen, that means that

If it is necessary that P is true, then P is true.

That is obviously correct. For epistemic logic, we replace the concept of *necessity* with the concept *know*. The new epistemic logic principle says:

If you know that P is true, then P is true.

That is obviously correct as well. You can't know something that is false. You might believe it, you might even believe it with all your heart, but you can't know it. The question then is, can we turn other modal principles concerning necessity and possibility into epistemological principles concerning knowledge and belief? Take the S5 (and S4) principle i above:

$$\Box P \to \Box\Box P$$

That principle says,

If it is necessary that P is true, then it is necessary that it is necessary that P is true.

For the equivalent in epistemic logic, we again replace the concept of *necessity* with the concept *know*. The new epistemic principle then says that.

If you know that P is true, then you know that you know that P is true.

This principle is controversial, and has generated enormous discussion.

Is that principle correct or not? Do you have to know that you know *P* in order to know *P*? That question will be left for you to think about.

Now an example from deontic logic. Let us start with the third basic principle above:

$$\Box P \to \sim \Diamond \sim P$$

That principle says,

If P is necessary, then it is not possible for P to be false.

For deontic logic, the concept *necessary* is replaced by the concept *obligatory*, and the concept *possible* is replaced by the concept *permissible*. Making those substitutions, the principle above becomes this:

If doing action P is obligatory, then it is not permissible not to do action P.

That seems exactly right. There is much more territory to explore in epistemic, deontic, and other similar logics. But you can see from this very brief discussion how various thinkers have tried to take advantage of progress made in modal logic by applying some of its logical structures and inferences in other areas.

VII. The Role of Modality

A great deal of work has been done in formal modal logic in recent decades, but philosophical interest in necessity and possibility goes back centuries. Why is this? One reason is that philosophers often see themselves as especially called to investigate necessary truths. Another reason is that historically, beginning with the Greeks, some philosophers have thought that the only things that can be truly known are necessary truths. Conceptual truths, analytic truths, logical truths, tautologies, correct fundamental principles of metaphysics, correct definitions, and the like are typically considered to be necessarily true. It should come as no surprise, then, that those things play a crucial role in philosophy. Furthermore, since in philosophy we often endeavor to discover necessary truths, explore the implications of necessary truths, and discern conceptual and logical connections between them, we have to know how to recognize necessary truths, how to reason about them, how to apply them, and how to integrate them into broader philosophical frameworks. And that's where formal modal logic comes into the picture.

If you browse through various philosophical topics, you will find that modal concepts and modal reasoning often play an essential role in philosophical argumentation. For instance, in trying to figure out what a human being is, Descartes argued that if it was *possible* for him to exist when his body did not, then he *had to be* distinct from his body, he *could not be* the same thing as his body (*Meditations* VI). Another example: when Thomas Aquinas developed his famous Five Ways in an attempt to prove that God exists, he appealed to modal principles in every single one of the Five Ways—for instance, that it was *impossible* for sequences of cause and effect to go back to infinity (*Summa theologiae* I-II,3). As it turns out, modality plays a particularly prominent role in philosophy of religion, which takes up such issues as God's existence, the concept of omnipotence, the definition of miracles, and so forth. Does God exist necessarily? Is it possible for God to do anything? Are miracles possible? In fact, there was an explosion of development in logic during the Middle Ages, and many historians of philosophy have claimed that the driving motivation was to develop more powerful and rigorous means for understanding God's various characteristics, how they are related to each other, and how God is related to the world. Odd as it may seem, religious interest was part of the explanation for the historical development of logic.

Modality plays an essential role in testing philosophical principles as well. As noted, fundamental philosophical principles are typically taken to be necessary truths—at least, correct philosophical principles are. But how do we tell whether we've gotten them right? In addition to developing supporting arguments for a certain claim, philosophers engage in conceptual testing. And just as automotive testing involves subjecting prototypes to extreme mechanical conditions, so testing proposed philosophical principles involves subjecting them to extreme conceptual conditions. We do that by trying to see whether they continue to hold up in logically demanding situations, and by looking for **counterexamples** to those principles. Remember that in possible-worlds language, if there is even *one* possible world, no matter how bizarre, in which some principle is false, then that principle cannot be a necessary truth. So philosophers try to find, imagine, or invent *possible* situations in which the principle in question would be false and is thus not *necessarily true*. The idea behind this kind of conceptual testing is simply an application of the modal principle that if P is *possibly* false, then P is not *necessarily* true, or in symbols:

$$\Diamond {\sim} P \rightarrow {\sim} \Box P$$

That principle is a direct consequence of the fourth basic principle stated above.

One famous example of conceptual testing comes from epistemology: the view that knowledge could be analyzed as justified true belief was revealed to be mistaken by contemporary American philosopher Edmund Gettier when he showed that it was *possible* in some odd circumstances for someone to have a justified true belief that did not constitute knowledge.

VIII. Modality and the Weirdness of Philosophy

You may have noticed (or you soon will) that philosophers tend to talk about weird stuff: What if you were really just a brain in a vat? What if aliens were manipulating all your choices? What if you were completely destroyed and then God created an exact duplicate of you—would that really be *you* again? The imaginations of philosophers often seem to be stuck in overdrive; they're constantly cooking up strange situations. Now we can get a glimpse of why that is the case. There are three factors in the explanation, and the first two in particular are connected to the role of modality just discussed.

First, there have been a lot of philosophers among the great minds of every period. Here are just a few examples: Aristotle (founder of logic, founder of biology), Descartes (inventor of analytic geometry), Leibniz (coinventor of calculus), Pascal (coinventor of modern probability theory), John Locke (whose political theory underpins most of America's founding documents), and others. And many people known primarily in other areas did some philosophical work as well, such as Robert Boyle (founder of modern chemistry) and Galileo (whose name is associated with the birth of modern physics). People of that caliber typically did not make trivial, obvious mistakes when they were thinking about philosophy, constructing philosophical arguments, defending specific philosophical principles, and the like. When they did get a bit off track, it was often in very subtle ways, which meant that testing, correcting, or rejecting their work involved digging deep, going far beyond the surface of the obvious. And that meant that searches for philosophical counterexamples frequently involved very odd, remote circumstances and possibilities.

Second, humans have been philosophizing for millennia. During that time, lots of mistakes have been identified. But over the millennia humans have remained concerned and curious about many of the same, persisting—or "perennial"—philosophical questions. So as the discussion continued and the obvious mistakes were identified, the subsequent mistakes got ever more subtle, ever more removed from surface matters. Unmasking deeper, subtler mistakes typically involves subjecting the argument or principle in question to ever more extreme conditions and tests—that is, to ever more bizarre possibilities. Again, any principle that is necessarily true must remain true in any possible circumstance—no matter how weird or strange.

So the very nature of the kind of truth—necessary truth—philosophy often seeks, the work of great minds that have historically been engaged in that effort, and the length of time the search has been going on, together drive at least some parts of philosophical discussion toward ever more remote conceptual possibilities. In fact, the more intuitively plausible or more reasonable sounding a proposed philosophical principle is, the weirder the possible circumstances that may be required to expose its weak points. Consequently, philosophers go to great lengths to imagine possibilities no one has ever seen or likely ever will see. And it's all connected to modal logic.

Third and finally, much of the weirdness of philosophy arises from the weirdness of philosophers themselves. Your own instructor in philosophy will no doubt strenuously deny being weird. And, we have to admit, there is at least one world in which your instructor is right. Maybe it's this one.

IX. Summary and Conclusion

Modal logic is an attempt to capture what we mean when we say that a statement is necessarily true, or possibly true, or not possibly true. It also traces out the kinds of inferences that are licensed by modal claims. As we've seen, the modalities of necessity and possibility play an important role across a wide range of philosophical issues and—as we saw in the conversation between Andrea and René—in thinking about significant everyday matters as well. Yet most of us are completely unaware of the modal principles that constitute a key part of the background to our reasoning. Indeed, even though they made use of some of its principles in an intuitive way, Andrea and René may not have known that they were depending upon modal logic or noticed when its most basic principles were violated. It would thus seem like a good idea for all of us to become more aware of the modal principles that underlie so much of our thought. Anyway, it couldn't hurt.

5.

Counterfactuals

"If I were president of this college . . ."

"Melissa," René interrupted, "if you were the president I would transfer to Fundamentals University yesterday."

"If I were president of this college," Melissa continued serenely, "I would declare the dorms *and* dorm rooms coed."

"You'd allow *dorm-shacking*?"—there was scandalized shock in René's voice.

"And," Melissa continued dreamily, "if coed rooms were permitted, I'd ask Keith to . . ."

"*What*!? But Keith, he . . . I mean . . . my . . . but . . . anyway Keith would never think of doing any such thing."

"Oh, uh, not the Keith you know, René," Melissa replied, just a shade too quickly. "This is a different one—one I just met in, um, my Postmodern Art class."

"Besides," Andrea chimed in, "if you were president of the college, you'd be old enough to be Keith's mother—or grandmother—50 at least, and no way would any 20-year-old guy want to . . ."

"No, no. I meant if coed rooms were permitted *now*, then I would . . . oh, never mind . . ." Melissa stopped mid-sentence, noting René's continuing distress—although whether that distress was over just the very idea of coed rooms or over the possibility that Melissa *did* mean the same Keith that René had a not-quite-secret crush on was not clear. In any case, at the mention of Keith, Andrea had given Melissa a weapons-grade warning look, and Melissa thought it best to drop the subject.

I. Counterfactuals: Basic Concepts

In the above conversation, there are several statements in the subjunctive mood—conditional statements of the general form:

> Were P true, then Q would be true.

For instance, Melissa tells her friends what she would do were she college president: she would open the dorms and dorm rooms to any gender roommate combinations. More formally (although perhaps a bit awkwardly):

> Were *Melissa is president* true, then *Melissa declares dorms and dorm rooms coed* would be true.

Similarly, René remarks in the subjunctive mood,

> Were *Melissa is president* true, then *René transfers to Fundamentals University* would be true.

Melissa again:

> Were *Dorms and dorm rooms are coed* true, then *Melissa asks Keith to be roommates* would be true.

Andrea also gets into the subjunctive act:

> Were *Melissa is president* true, then *Melissa is at least 50 and Keith is not interested in Melissa* would be true.

And, finally, Melissa changes focus slightly:

> Were *Dorms and dorm rooms are coed here and now* true, then *Melissa asks Keith to be roommates* would be true.

It should be evident from the foregoing discussion of coed dorms that subjunctive conditionals are familiar conversational resources. We use them quite often. They expand the scope of our knowledge to what would be true if things were different. Subjunctives are used in a number of ways. Often they are used to explore implications and aspects of possible situations (past, present, or future) whose actual occurrence is in doubt or dispute. Sometimes they involve hypothetical situations that do not exist at the moment, are known not to exist, and perhaps never did and never will exist. Melissa is not president of the college and almost certainly (René hopes) never will be. René has not transferred to Fundamentals University and likely never will. Subjunctive conditionals that contain antecedents that are not in fact true are referred to as *contrary-to-fact conditionals* or, more commonly, either *counterfactual conditionals* or simply **counterfactuals**.

Counterfactuals are important not only in everyday discussions but in nearly every academic discipline as well. One frequently encounters statements such as the following in the relevant disciplinary contexts:

- Were the European Union to collapse, then US economic growth would slow.
- Were the gravitational constant significantly different than it actually is, then there would be no life in the cosmos.
- Were Hitler to have won WWII, then a good part of the world would be at the mercy of violent psychopaths.
- Were Shakespeare to have been an illiterate animal herder, then we would never have to read *Hamlet* in high school.

Counterfactual claims can be made in a wide variety of ways. For example:

- Had the meteor not struck at the end of the Cretaceous Age, dinosaurs would now rule the world.
- If we lacked free will, then some influential explanations for the existence of evil would not work.
- Suppose that you had won the Powerball lottery—you'd be rich.
- The environment would be in better shape had the gasoline engine not been invented.

The above claims involve exploration of nonactual possibilities and proposed implications of those nonactual possibilities, what we might expect *if* those things had become realities or did become realities. But sometimes the antecedent turns out to be true. We just didn't know it was true at the time we were speculating about it. And sometimes it becomes true. René and Andrea may come back for their 30-year class reunion, only to make the appalling discovery that Melissa has just been named the new president. (Do you suppose that at age 50 she will still favor coed dorm rooms?) But even in cases where the antecedent of a subjunctive is true, many philosophers still employ the term *counterfactual*.

II. Analyzing Counterfactuals Logically: Preliminary Attempts

How should we construe the logic of counterfactual claims? It would seem that counterfactuals depend upon some sort of *connection* between antecedent and consequent in a conditional statement. Consider this counterfactual:

> A. Had you chosen a different college than you in fact did, then you would have turned into a tadpole.

The antecedent of that counterfactual seems utterly irrelevant to the consequent. There is just no plausible connection whatever. Consequently, we take *A* to be obviously false. (If it is in fact true, then during the time that you almost decided to go to a different college, you had a very narrow escape.)

What kind of connection, then, what sort of logical link between antecedent and consequent is required in order for a counterfactual to be true? The answer, one might reasonably think, is obvious. Material conditionals (conditionals as defined by the truth table for conditionals) were already introduced in the chapter on deductive logic, as were their functions in various syllogistic forms—hypothetical syllogism, modus ponens, modus tollens, and the like. Why not simply treat counterfactual conditionals as standard material conditionals as defined by the truth table?

IIa: Material Conditionals?

As it turns out, that suggestion doesn't work. The truth table for material conditionals depends almost exclusively upon the individual truth-values of the antecedent and consequent regardless of whether or not they are connected to each other at all. Thus any "connection" between antecedent and consequent in a material conditional can be so weak as to be nonexistent. Here are just two ways in which the material conditional fails our intuitions. First, according to the truth table, a material conditional is automatically true whenever its antecedent is false. Since counterfactual *A* above has a false antecedent, the truth table for material conditionals pronounces *A* to be true—which it clearly is not. Second, according to that truth table, material conditionals are always true when both antecedent and consequent are true. But counterfactuals don't work that way either. Think about this counterfactual:

> B. Were there now a hole in the ozone layer above Antarctica, then Caesar would have chosen to cross the Rubicon several centuries ago.

In this case, both the antecedent and the consequent are true. But that counterfactual borders on downright nonsense.

In both *A* and *B*, the antecedent and consequent have no connection. Neither *A* nor *B* seems true. Yet in both cases the truth table, requiring no relevant connections whatever between antecedent and consequent, happily pronounces them true. The material conditional thus fails to give us a plausible interpretation of counterfactuals. We need some other way of thinking about the proper connection between antecedent and consequent in counterfactual claims.

What exactly is the proper sort of connection? What type of connection should we look for before we accept a counterfactual as true? If truth tables are inadequate, what other possible types of connections might there be between antecedents and consequents?

IIB. INDICATIVE CONDITIONALS?

Indicative conditionals are conditionals in which a specific part of the antecedent is taken as a truth already fixed in the context. Suppose that cigarette smoke in the dorm laundry room sets off a fire alarm. Suspicion turns, naturally, toward Melissa. But Melissa, just as naturally, denies all guilt. In this situation, it is a fixed given that the alarm was in fact set off, so the following indicative conditional seems true:

> C. If Melissa didn't set off the fire alarm, then someone else did.

The alarm being set off is a given, the only question is, who did it? But the corresponding subjunctive does not seem to be true. There is no reason whatever to believe that,

D. If Melissa hadn't set off the fire alarm, then someone else would have.

Given that *C* and *D* have essentially the same antecedents and consequents, the fact that one is true and the other false shows that counterfactuals and indicative conditionals are not the same thing. We must look further.

IIc. Logical Entailment?

Another possible type of connection was discussed in the chapter on modal logic —a logically necessary connection (or logical entailment):

Necessarily (if *P* is true, then *Q* is true).

But this won't work either. Whereas the material conditional is too weak to represent counterfactuals, logically necessary connections are in general too strong for counterfactuals. Recall the very first example of a counterfactual statement at the beginning of the chapter:

E. Were the European Union to collapse, then US economic growth would slow.

While *E* is very likely true, there is no rule of pure logic, nor is there any necessarily true metaphysical link or conceptually necessary link, connecting an EU collapse to a slowdown in US growth. However unlikely, it is logically possible that the EU collapse and US growth not shrink at all. So logical necessity is not the right sort of connection.

IId. Causal Connections?

Another alternative involves causal connections. Perhaps the required connection between antecedent and consequent in a true counterfactual involves causal laws, laws of nature, natural principles of cause and effect. Think for a moment about Newton's view of gravitation—that every chunk of matter attracts every other chunk of matter (in a precisely specified way). Assuming for the moment that Newton was right on this point, that universal pattern of gravitation is not just a coincidence, it is backed up by the way nature is structured to operate. In some sense that pattern governs the way chunks of matter *must* behave. But here the "must" is not a matter of logical necessity. Nature didn't have to be structured according to that pattern. In order to distinguish the "must" of natural laws from logical necessity, the "must" in this case is typically referred to as *nomic necessity* or *nomological necessity*. Nevertheless, given the natural law of gravitation, we can make the following claim:

> F. *Were* some entirely new chunk of matter to suddenly pop into existence, then it too *would* obey the law of gravitational attraction.

F is based on the law of gravitation. In fact, it's an application of the law of gravitation. It is also a counterfactual claim. Natural laws cover not only things, events, and processes that *do* exist, they say something about how things *would* go even in situations that don't in fact obtain. That is what philosophers mean when they say that natural laws support counterfactuals (or support subjunctives).

Although this "causal connection" alternative does tell some part of the story concerning the type of connections we seek, it is not the whole story. Counterfactual *E* seems true, but just as there is no logical law stipulating that connection, there does not seem to be any causal law, any law of nature that would connect the fate of the EU and the US economy in the way indicated by *E* above. So we still need to look a bit further.

III. Digging Deeper: Possible-Worlds Semantics

Although lots of questions remain unanswered, significant insights into counterfactuals have been achieved by employing the idea of possible worlds, which was introduced in section II of the chapter on modal logic. Most of the key early applications of possible worlds to counterfactuals are attributed to the contemporary philosopher Robert Stalnaker, although others (like David Lewis, Alvin Plantinga, and Bas van Fraassen) have made important contributions to this line of thinking.

Let's begin tracking Stalnaker's initial basic insight by way of a simple example. Think about the following counterfactual:

> G. Were Thomas Aquinas to have been born into a poor family, then the *Summa theologiae* would never have been written.

According to Stalnaker, when we intuitively evaluate a counterfactual like that for truth, we first imagine a situation (a possible world) in which, rather than being born into a highly placed, wealthy family (as he in fact was), Aquinas was born into a poor one. To make things easier, let's call our actual world α and this other world, in which Aquinas is born poor, β. There are zillions of *possible* worlds in which Aquinas is born poor—some very like ours, some sort of like ours, some wildly different from ours, as well as everything in between and beyond. Among all those different possible worlds in which Aquinas is born poor, Stalnaker asks us to think of the one that is still the *most like ours* – the *closest* similar world, the *nearest* similar world in which that birth into poverty occurs. In effect, we think of a world like our actual world *except* that in that other world the antecedent of the counterfactual is *true*. World β would thus be as like α as possible except for the key change: the financial circumstances of Aquinas's family. In most respects α and β are nearly identical. The overwhelming majority of things in β have no relevance to the circumstances of Aquinas's birth and thus are unchanged from α—natural laws, geography, virtually all of history, your favorite color of socks, the chemical makeup of nylon, the number of stars in the M81 galaxy, the vapidity of prime time American television, your instructor's incomprehensible refusal to give you more points on the last exam, the percentage of carbon in the steel used in Toyotas. All things unrelated to Aquinas's birth will be the same in both α and β.

There will have to be some prior background adjustments necessary for the proposed change to be incorporated into β, adjustments required in order to accommodate the counterfactual change (in this case, Aquinas's family being poor). Clearly, the prior events that in our world α were responsible for Aquinas's family being wealthy when he was born would have to have gone differently in counterfactual world β. That is a requirement for Aquinas's financial circumstances being different. That adjustment, and others, are required just in order to fit the change—a poor family—consistently into world β. On Stalnaker's theory we imagine the antecedent true and make whatever background adjustments are required in order for the antecedent to be true. But we make the fewest changes we can in order to keep β still as nearly like α as possible despite the changes.

More importantly, the primary counterfactual change will lead to consequences downstream. In our case, the consequences will most likely affect the opportunities Aquinas would get, the education Aquinas would be able to receive, the prospects of his coming to the attention of influential clerics and scholars, his receiving the support necessary to write the

Summa theologiae, and so forth. But now we ask: In this changed world β, will those changes—the necessary background adjustments leading up to the antecedent and the consequences that result from the antecedent—result in β differing from α on the point of Aquinas never writing the *Summa theologiae*? Are the *connections* between the circumstances of his birth and his becoming the author of *Summa theologiae* such that a real-world change in the first part (circumstances of birth) will result in a change in the second part (authorship of the *Summa*)? If it does, then the counterfactual is true. If not, then it is false.

In this case, as in many counterfactual cases, it may be difficult or impossible to tell for sure. Would Aquinas in poverty never have acquired the education, resources, and opportunities to develop into the theologian and author we know today? Or would his talents have been so extraordinary that they would have been recognized regardless of his lowly birth? Would he have been lifted out of his impoverished family situation and written the *Summa theologiae* anyway? Although establishing the truth or falsehood of counterfactual *G* may be utterly beyond us, on Stalnaker's theory these are the kind of questions we would have to ask in order to assess the truth of counterfactual claims.

IV. Stalnaker's Theory

In a nutshell, then, Stalnaker's idea is this:

S₁: The counterfactual *If P were true then Q would be true* is true if and only if: in the nearest possible world, the possible world most like the real world but in which the antecedent *P* is true, the consequent *Q* is true as well.

S₂: The counterfactual *If P were true then Q would be true* is false just in case: in the nearest possible world, the possible world most like the real world but in which the antecedent *P* is true, the consequent *Q* is false.

Strictly speaking, **S₁** and **S₂** are logically equivalent, but it is sometimes helpful to have both explicitly stated. Think about an earlier example:

H. Were Hitler to have won WWII, then a good part of the world would be at the mercy of violent psychopaths.

Well, in the world most like ours but in which the antecedent is true (Hitler won), then, given what we know of Hitler and his Nazi cohorts, is the consequent true (many are at the mercy of violent psychopaths)? If yes—which seems pretty plausible—then *H* is true.

Let's take another example from the beginning of the chapter:

> I. Were Shakespeare to have been an illiterate animal herder, then we never would have to read *Hamlet* in high school.

In the world most like ours but in which Shakespeare was an illiterate animal herder, are people excused from reading *Hamlet* in high school? That's hard to say. Some people argue that even in this world Shakespeare did not write the works attributed to him. If so, then even in the nearest world in which he was illiterate, those works would have been written anyway by whoever actually did write them, and thus the people in that world would *still* have had *Hamlet* in their high school book bag—in which case that counterfactual would be false.

V. Melissa and Dorm Policies

Let's apply Stalnaker's idea to the opening discussion of coed dorms. Recall the first counterfactual in that discussion:

> J. Were *Melissa is president* true, then *Melissa declares dorms and dorm rooms coed* would be true.

Here's the cognitive process we go through in evaluating this claim for truth. We picture to ourselves a situation (a possible world) as exactly similar to the actual world as possible except for changes required to make the antecedent of *J* true—that is, a world in which *Melissa is president* is true. Melissa herself assures us that in that counterfactual situation there would be an additional important consequent difference: she would institute a coed dorm and dorm room policy. Melissa is thus imagining a situation in which although there are important differences (viz., her presidency), one feature of the present situation that would remain constant in both situations would be her preferences and intentions with respect to dorm policy (and Keith), and that she would thus use her powers as college president to bring it about that the consequent of *J*, *Melissa declares dorms and dorm rooms coed*, would also then be made true. If that is correct, then counterfactual *J* itself is true.

Granted, altering the original situation so that Melissa is president would require some additional background adjustments. For instance, we know from experience that in worlds like ours, 20-year-old students are not appointed as college presidents. So when considering a world just like the actual world except Melissa is president of the college, Andrea automatically takes the fact about college presidents in the actual world into account. Andrea then holds that feature of the actual world constant in the new situation as well, and incorporates that constant pattern concerning ages of presidents from the actual world into the new situation. She then points out the implication that in the nearest world where Melissa was president (where the antecedent *Melissa is president* is true), one additional related change is that Melissa would be at least 50 years old, not her current 20, which was what Melissa seemed to be dreaming about. And when Andrea points out this implied age adjustment connected with Melissa's presidency, René and Melissa immediately understand why that change would be part of the new situation. Melissa then switches her focus to a *new* counterfactual situation, one in which dorm policies are already changed *here and now* but is just like the actual situation with respect to her current age.

VI. A Significant Complexity: "Pragmatic Ambiguity"

Stalnaker's basic idea (S_1, S_2) seems relatively straightforward. But there is a deep complication lurking just below the surface. Think about this claim:

> K. The environment would be in better shape had the gasoline engine not been invented.

Is that true? The internal combustion gasoline engine is responsible for a significant amount of the CO_2 and other pollutants that are driving climate change and other untoward trends in the natural environment. So without the millions and millions of automotive pollution sources on our highways, the environment would surely be in better shape. So *K* seems to be true.

But, on the other hand, our present world contains millions and millions of vehicles, around which economies, cities, nations, lifestyles, and demographic patterns are built. Were it not for the internal combustion gasoline engine, those vehicles would be powered by heavily polluting coal-fired steam engines and who knows what else, and the environmental situation would surely be vastly worse than it is now. Thus, in the nearest world in which the gasoline engine was never invented, the environmental situation would be worse, not better. So *K* seems to be false.

Both stories seem plausible. But how can that be, since they contradict each other? The answer has to do with how *similarity*, or *nearness*, or *closeness* of possible worlds is judged. When we ask whether some object *a* is more similar to *b* than it is to *c*, we have to make that comparative judgment in terms of certain *respects* of similarity. For instance, an apple is more similar to a stop sign than to a banana with respect to color, but an apple is more similar to a banana than to a stop sign with respect to edibility. Two things are similar in a specific respect when they share a relevant property in common. Thus, an apple and a stop sign are similar in both having the property of redness. The apple and banana are similar in both having the property of edibility. So when we ask, "Is an apple more similar to a stop sign or to a banana?," we have to stipulate a specific property in terms of which that question is to be answered. Are we asking for similarity in color terms or in dietary terms? Without that stipulation, questions of similarity are ambiguous. It's hard to know how to answer them. One person, having one respect of similarity in mind, might see things one way, whereas a different person, having a different respect of similarity in mind, might see things in a different way. Until they both understand what respects of similarity are at issue, they may simply be talking past each other. In the case of the apple, one person may be thinking *color*, thus claiming that the stop sign is more similar to the apple, whereas the other, thinking *edibility*, says that the banana is more similar. Not realizing the difference in their criteria, each of them might think that the other person is totally loony.

The same principle applies to comparisons of similarity among possible worlds. World α may be more similar to world β than it is to world γ in some respects, but more similar to world γ than it is to world β in some other respects. For example, world α may be closer to (i.e., more similar to, more like) world β than to world γ in terms of the dominant forms of government, but closer to (i.e., more similar to, more like) world γ than to world β in terms of the average standard of living in the southern hemisphere—or in terms of the number of penguin species, or of the scientific progress made since 1750, or any of a vast array of other respects. Thus, when we think about one possible world being closer to our world, the actual world, than some other possible world, that close-ness must always be defined in terms of properties that the closer world will share with the actual world.

But frequently the relevant respects in which similarity is to be judged are not explicitly specified, and confusion can result when different peo-ple assume different criteria of similarity between worlds. Which alter-native world is considered to be more similar to the actual world depends upon the similarity criteria in question, and such criteria are typically de-termined by the context and the intentions of the people involved in the discussion. In short, the selection is purely a *pragmatic* matter. Whether a specific counterfactual is true or false depends upon the criteria of similarity, and its truth-value can change when those criteria change; additionally, the choice of criteria depends upon the contexts and inten-tions of the people involved. Because of this, there is no simple right or wrong here. It simply depends on the pragmatic features of the context. Thus, subjunctives are said to be *pragmatically ambiguous*.

The idea of pragmatic ambiguity may sound a bit daunting, but we work with it intuitively all the time, even in ordinary occasions such as the discussion about coed dorms. As we saw, Melissa was keeping her age constant. That was one of her criteria for similarity of the relevant counterfactual world to this world. Andrea, on the other hand, kept con-stant the general truth that college presidents are never 20-year-olds, but usually at least 50. That was one of her criteria for similarity of the relevant counterfactual world to this world. And that difference had sig-nificant implications for whether Keith would likely agree to be Melissa's roommate. In the world Melissa was thinking of as most similar to the actual world, perhaps he would; but he very likely would not in the world Andrea was thinking of as most similar to the actual world. What are or are not implicitly taken to be common features when determining simi-larity of worlds is thus crucial in evaluating the truth of a counterfactual.

In the case of the gasoline engine, if we are thinking of similarity in terms of keeping the total number of vehicles the same in both worlds, then K seems false (the engine replacements might be worse). If we are thinking of similarity in terms of keeping the fact that gasoline engines are the main producer of vehicular pollution the same in both worlds, then K seems true (the major source was gasoline engines, but now they are absent).

Although it has some complexities, Stalnaker's approach to counter-factuals seems intuitively plausible. Like other parts of logic, it seems to capture our natural ways of thinking. Since Stalnaker's initial proposal in

1968 there have been other proposals in the area of counterfactual logic, but nearly all of them have been extensions of or variations on Stalnaker's original idea.

VII. Counterfactual Reasoning

We turn now to broader questions concerning the use of counterfactuals in logical argumentation.

VIIA. CONDITIONALS AND VALIDITY.

As we've seen, counterfactuals do not act like material conditionals. In fact, it may have occurred to you that virtually no conditionals used in either ordinary or philosophical discourse behave in the way material conditionals do. For instance, we almost never take the falsehood of an antecedent to guarantee the truth of the whole conditional, although that is how material conditionals work. Yet, when we evaluate most arguments for validity—hypothetical syllogisms and such—the conditionals in those arguments are treated as if they were material conditionals. Does that mean that the sort of logic employed not only in the chapter on deductive logic but also in most philosophy classrooms is basically bogus? No. As it turns out, for an enormous range of both ordinary and technical arguments, if the conditionals involved are *treated* as material conditionals for purposes of evaluating the validity of the argument in question, the normal methods of deductive logic will produce the right answer. Interpreting a counterfactual as a material conditional will not always produce a reliable answer as to whether that conditional is true, but the question of whether an argument is *valid* and the question of whether or a statement involved in the argument is actually *true* are distinct—indeed, nearly unrelated—questions. So using a truth table is not a good way to tell if an ordinary conversational or philosophical *conditional* is true. But it is part of a good way to tell if an ordinary conversational or philosophical *argument* is valid, at least for an enormous range of arguments.

VIIв. Counterfactuals and Valid Standard Argument Forms

Although counterfactuals are very different from other sorts of conditionals, many of the argument forms you are familiar with are also valid for counterfactuals.

1. Modus ponens
For instance, recall modus ponens:

$$1. \; A \rightarrow B$$
$$2. \; A$$
$$/ \therefore \quad 3. \; B$$

The same form is also valid when the conditional is a counterfactual. There is no universally accepted standard symbol for counterfactual conditionals, so let's use "~»" since it has the great virtue of being reproducible by most word processing programs. So the following argument is valid:

	1. Were *P* true, then *Q* would be true.	1.	$P \sim\!\!» Q$
	2. *P* is in fact true.	2.	P
So:	3. *Q* is in fact true.	$/ \therefore$ 3.	Q

The validity of that argument can be shown in terms of possible worlds. Translated into possible-worlds talk, the argument goes like this:

1. In the nearest possible world in which *P* is true, then *Q* is true in that world as well.
2. *P* is true in the actual world (is in fact true).

So: 3. *Q* is true in the actual world (is in fact true).

Now, if *P* is true in fact, in the actual world, then the actual world will be the world most similar to the actual world in which *P* is true. After all (and this is an important principle):

No world can be more like the actual world than the actual world itself.

In technical terms, this is called the *centering assumption*. But in that nearest world where *P* is true, *Q* will be true as well, according to the first premise. So since the actual world is that nearest world, Q will be true in the actual world—exactly what the conclusion says.

2. Modus tollens

If you think through what the premises and conclusion say in terms of possible worlds, you will also be able to see that modus tollens is a valid form for counterfactuals:

$$
\begin{array}{rll}
1. & P \sim\!\!» Q \\
2. & \sim\!Q \\
/ \therefore 3. & \sim\!P
\end{array}
$$

A partial list of valid counterfactual argument forms is found in section VIII.

VIIc. Hints of Logical Difficulty

However, not all familiar argument forms work for counterfactuals. The hypothetical syllogism is one example. Think about the following argument (from Edmund Gettier). Imagine that you are the third and last child born to your parents. It thus seems true that

1. Had you not been born, then your parents would have had exactly two children.

It also seems true in general that

2. Had your parents never existed, then you would not have been born.

As we know, the hypothetical syllogism is a deductively valid argument form for ordinary conditionals. Thus, if (1) and (2) above are treated as ordinary conditionals, we should be able to conclude as the result of a deductively valid argument that

3. Had your parents never existed, then your parents would have had exactly two children.

Something has gone dreadfully wrong here. The conditions specified in (1) and (2) seem true, whereas (3) is outrageously false. The argument thus fits the classic definition of invalidity despite appearing to be an instance of the perfectly valid hypothetical syllogism form. Not good. That means that hypothetical syllogism is not a valid argument form for counterfactuals.

3. Counterfactual Hypothetical Syllogism

There is, however, a very similar form that is valid for counterfactuals:

$$
\begin{array}{rl}
1. & P \sim\!\!\!\gg Q \\
2. & (P \wedge Q) \sim\!\!\!\gg R \\
/ \therefore \; 3. & P \sim\!\!\!\gg R
\end{array}
$$

We may call this *counterfactual hypothetical syllogism.* One of the exercises for this chapter involves explaining in terms of possible worlds why that is valid—why, that is, if (1) in the nearest world in which P is true then Q is true, and (2) in the nearest world in which both P and Q are true then R is true, then it must also be the case that (3) in the nearest world in which P is true then R is also true.

VIII. Some Valid Subjunctive Arguments

The following argument forms are valid in nearly all subjunctive theories:

1. Modus ponens
$$
\begin{array}{rl}
1. & P \sim\!\!\!\gg Q \\
2. & P \\
/ \therefore \; 3. & Q
\end{array}
$$

2. Modus tollens
$$
\begin{array}{rl}
1. & P \sim\!\!\!\gg Q \\
2. & \sim Q \\
/ \therefore \; 3. & \sim P
\end{array}
$$

3. Counterfactual HS
$$
\begin{array}{rl}
1. & P \sim\!\!\!\gg Q \\
2. & (P \wedge Q) \sim\!\!\!\gg R \\
/ \therefore \; 3. & P \sim\!\!\!\gg R
\end{array}
$$

4. Mixed modal HS
$$
\begin{array}{rl}
1. & P \sim\!\!\!\gg Q \\
2. & \Box(Q \wedge R) \\
/ \therefore \; 3. & P \sim\!\!\!\gg R
\end{array}
$$

5. Distribution 1   1. $(P \vee Q) \sim\!\!» R$

       / $\therefore$ 2. $(P \sim\!\!» R) \vee (Q \sim\!\!» R)$

The following are valid in most, but not all, counterfactual theories, and all are in fact controversial.

6. Impossible antecedents   1. $\sim\!\Diamond P$

       / $\therefore$ 2. $P \sim\!\!» Q$

According to this inference form, *any* subjunctive with a necessarily false (i.e., impossible) antecedent is true no matter what the consequent is—and no matter whether there is any connection between antecedent and consequent. Since that seems to violate a very basic intuition concerning counterfactuals, some philosophers reject the inference.

7. True/True thesis   1. $P \wedge Q$

       / $\therefore$ 2. $P \sim\!\!» Q$

If P and Q are both true in the actual world, then the actual world is the nearest world in which P is true, and Q is true in that (actual) world as well, making the counterfactual true as well on Stalnaker's theory. However, that does not seem correct to many people (see counterfactual B earlier in this chapter). Some theories (e.g., some of David Lewis's) avoid this implication.

8. Counterfactual negation   1. $\sim\!(P \sim\!\!» Q)$

       / $\therefore$ 2. $P \sim\!\!» \sim\!Q$

9. Distribution 2   1. $P \sim\!\!» (Q \vee R)$

       / $\therefore$ 2. $(P \sim\!\!» Q) \vee (P \sim\!\!» R)$

IX. Some Subjunctive Fallacies

The following argument forms, while all valid for material conditionals, are *invalid* in nearly all subjunctive theories.

1. Hypothetical syllogism   1. $A \sim\!\!» B$

            2. $B \sim\!\!» C$

       / $\therefore$ 3. $A \sim\!\!» C$

As discussed, there is a variant—counterfactual hypothetical syllogism—that is valid.

2. Contraposition

Although contraposition:

> 1. $P \rightarrow Q$
> $/ \therefore$ 2. $\sim Q \rightarrow \sim P$

is a valid form for the material conditional, its counterfactual counterpart,

> 1. $P \sim\!\!» Q$
> $/ \therefore$ 2. $\sim Q \sim\!\!» \sim P$

is not valid. The reason for the failure of contraposition may not be obvious at first glance, so here is an example. Suppose that René decides to transfer to Fundamentals University regardless of whether Melissa were president. Thus:

>   a. Were Melissa president, then René would transfer.
> and
>   b. Were Melissa not president, then René would transfer.

are both true. But now consider the counterfactual contrapositive of b:

>   c. Were René not to transfer, then Melissa would be president.

That, of course, is not true. Thus, although (b) is true, its contrapositive (c) is not. So although contraposition works for material conditionals, it does not always work for counterfactual conditionals.

3. Strengthening

Any addition to the antecedent of a true material conditional leaves that truth-value unchanged. That is,

> 1. $P \rightarrow Q$
> $/ \therefore$ 2. $(P \wedge R) \rightarrow Q$

is a valid argument form for the material conditional, no matter what proposition R is. But the same does not work with counterfactuals, and

$$1.\ P \sim\!\!» Q$$
$$/\therefore\ 2.\ (P \wedge R) \sim\!\!» Q$$

is in fact invalid. Consider one of the initial counterfactuals:

L. Were *Melissa is president* true, then *René transfers to Fundamentals University* would be true.

Suppose we make this addition to the antecedent:

M. Were *Melissa is president* **and Melissa is a shining beacon of virtue, understanding, and good sense** true, then *René transfers to Fundamentals University* would be true.

Intuitively, the reason is that the nearest world in which P is true may very well not be the nearest world in which $(P \wedge R)$ is true, and thus while Q may be true in the former world (as in counterfactual L), there is no guarantee that it will be true in the latter world (as in counterfactual M). Indeed, were the president of her school a shining beacon of virtue, understanding, and good sense, René would likely *not* transfer.

X. Summary and Conclusion

Counterfactual reasoning typically deals with the implications of statements concerning states of affairs that, as far as we know, do not exist. We make use of this kind of reasoning when we think about what would have happened if the past had been different; what would be the case if the present were different; and what will happen in the future under certain imagined scenarios. Counterfactuals are familiar; they are indispensable for the way we reason about the world; and they are complex. This chapter has dealt with what may seem like horrible complications, and indeed it is one of the most difficult chapters in the book.

Still, we have not gone very far beneath the surface of counterfactuals. There are a number of different theories of counterfactuals, each exhibiting subtle differences in what counterfactuals mean, which counterfactuals are true or false, and what inferences involving counterfactual claims are legitimate. And there are other types of conditionals we have not considered—for instance, "might" conditionals (*Were P true, then Q **might** be true*), counterpossible conditionals (conditionals having necessarily false antecedents, yet still seeming to be false), counterlegal conditionals (conditionals with antecedents contrary to laws of nature), and so on. There is still a lot of territory to be explored, lots of issues to be resolved, and lots of important philosophical arguments that depend upon as-yet poorly understood aspects of counterfactuals and other kinds of conditionals.

But that unexplored territory constitutes an opportunity. Just think. *Were* you to pursue a career in philosophy, then you *might* become the one to go down in history as having finally solved the deep puzzles of counterfactuals. And *were* that to happen, then Melissa, the president of your college, *would* surely give you a huge raise.

6.

Inductive Arguments

"I don't mean to be critical, Melissa—well, actually I do—but of all the millions of stupid things you've ever done, this is the absolute, abysmally *stupidest*. It's a SCAM."

"Look, you wouldn't think so if you would just read her e-mail. She's a really devout woman struggling in poverty and just wants a little help from a fellow believer. And it isn't her fault that her greedy government wants to steal her father's inheritance from her. All she wants to do is to transfer the money to my bank account where it will be safe, and then I'll get 25% of it. And I can use it—I've already got about $27,000 in student loans, and tuition is going up again, of course."

"Melissa—it's a *scam*. Everybody on the planet knows it's a scam. If there are any Martians, all of them know it's a scam. How on earth could you be taken in by anything so obviously phony?"

"You're always so harsh and judgmental. Not to mention suspicious. Anyway, Andrea, you're the one who's always harping about only believing things if you have evidence. So how can you just decree that it's a scam without even bothering to read the e-mail she sent?"

"Because scammers send out millions of e-mails exactly like that, and all of them have always turned out to be rip-offs. Once they get your account information, they simply clean out your account and you never hear from them again. Have you checked your account balance since you did this?"

I. Induction: Basic Concepts

It won't come as a surprise to anyone that Melissa is going to need an even bigger student loan for the coming semester than she had anticipated. (And it is pretty obvious that neither Andrea nor Melissa has read the section in the ethics of argument chapter below concerning how to treat discussion partners.)

In the exchange over the e-mail call for help, both Andrea and Melissa have been engaging in **enumerative induction**. This type of argument goes by a variety of names: *generalization, inductive generalization,* or simply *induction.* Inductive reasoning involves projecting specific patterns we have become familiar with into other areas, including the future. We reason this way almost constantly. It comes so naturally to us that we are often not even aware that we're doing it.

In the case above, Andrea was arguing that there was a very familiar and invariable pattern:

> 1. All of the many cases of e-mail of the sort Melissa just received have so far turned out to be scams.
>
> Therefore,
>
> 2. Probably the present case—Melissa's e-mail—will turn out to be a scam as well.

Most of us would find Andrea's argument convincing. You yourself have probably deleted lots of such e-mail messages without reading them because you have intuitively, almost automatically, and perhaps even unconsciously constructed Andrea's inductive argument. Some people have not been quite so logically adept and have consequently fallen for the scam.

This is the way inductive reasoning goes:

> 1. We have a *sample* of cases of the type in question; these are the cases that we already know about (in the case above, the e-mails asking for bank account numbers).
> 2. We see a specific *pattern* that all the cases within that sample exhibit and know of no cases that violate that pattern (the e-mails were all scams).

Then,

> 3. By inference we *project* that pattern onto the present case

(Melissa's current e-mail is likely a scam as well), or onto the next case, or onto all other cases of the type of thing in question. We infer that other cases will exhibit the same pattern we see within the cases already known.

The structure of inductive inference can be characterized more formally in this way:

1. All the cases of type *T* with which we are already familiar have characteristic *C*.

Therefore,

2. Probably the *present* case (or the *next* case, or all *other* cases) of type *T* will have characteristic *C*.

As indicated, inductive conclusions may be about the current case or the next case we come across or even all such cases—past, present, and future. Typically we do not yet know the details of those cases. In inductive inferences with regard to the future we are making a prediction on the basis of prior experience that a pattern we have observed to this point will continue, that the cases we encounter in the future will exhibit the same pattern we have seen in the past. For that reason you will often see induction characterized in terms of the principle that *the future will be like the past* in specified respects. But, as many have pointed out (most notably the Scottish philosopher David Hume, 1711–1776), we don't have any *deductive* guarantee that patterns in the past will continue into the future. That's why, no matter how strong the evidence, inductive conclusions are only *probable*. Although it is overwhelmingly probable that Melissa's e-mail is a scam, it is still *possible* that she may have actually gotten the single e-mail in the entire history of the planet that violates the pattern and isn't a scam. But don't bet on it.

(A terminological note: what is called "mathematical induction" is actually a type of deduction and is not discussed here.)

II. The Importance of Induction

Inductive generalizations constitute an important part of everyday reasoning, be it conscious or unconscious. When you buy a new bottle of Advil you do so implicitly inferring that the tablets in this new bottle will cure minor aches and pains because that's been the familiar pattern up to this point. When you download a new song by your favorite group, you anticipate enjoying the new song on the basis of a pattern of enjoyment that held in the past. In fact, you regularly stake your life on thousands of inductions you've never explicitly thought about—for instance, on the induction that your next pizza, like all your past pizzas, will not be lethal; that when you step on the brakes, your car will stop; that your even-tempered and gentle dog will be even-tempered and gentle the next time you see him.

More fundamentally, we anticipate the continuance of a wide variety of patterns in nature because nature has exhibited those patterns throughout the past. You anticipate being able to walk outside without flying off the planet. You don't expect to see the sun rise in the west. You have never worried about the floor under you dematerializing and dumping you into the basement. You've never lost sleep over the idea that your left earlobe might detonate in the middle of the night. Why not, in those cases? After all, they are *logically* possible. How can you be so utterly confident that those things aren't actually going to happen? The answer: because they've never happened before. We infer inductively from familiar patterns in past experience that such things just don't—and won't—happen.

Not only our ordinary common sense thinking, but our scientific thinking too rests in part on inductive inferences. Scientific principles, theories and conclusions frequently involve general claims—that under standard conditions water always boils at 100°C, that all electrons have a rest mass of 9.1×10^{-31} kg; that all cows have four stomachs; that all copper conducts electricity; that chemical reactions that occur in a lab on Tuesday in New Jersey will, under the same conditions, yield the same results in a cosmetics factory on Friday in China; that the natural laws that hold here and now are the laws for all of nature; and on and on.

We have observed only a vanishingly small fraction of all past and present water in the cosmos, a vanishingly small fraction of all electrons, of all cows, of all copper. So how in science do we get to principles about *all* electrons, *all* cows, *all* copper? Those universal conclusions result in part from inductively extending patterns we observe now in our corner of the universe to all other parts of the universe, past, present, and future. And a good part of the basis for that inference is the inductive assumption that the fundamental patterns that nature exhibits in our experience also hold for nature's behavior beyond our experience. In the scientific context, this principle of pattern stability—that nature in the future will be like nature in the past in specified respects—is referred to as *the principle of the uniformity of nature* (briefly discussed in the chapter on scientific inference).

So we are constantly engaging in inductive reasoning: from simple and largely unconscious inductions about our next pizza not being lethal, to certain e-mails being scams, to such massive inductions as that every single bit of unexamined copper in the universe—from billions of years in the past to the entire future of the cosmos and from your back yard to entire galaxies billions of light-years away—will conduct electricity. Given the frequency and importance of inductions, we would do well to consider when we should—and when we should not—accept such arguments and depend upon their conclusions.

III. Evaluating Inductive Arguments

As with other argument types, there are good inductions and bad inductions. In some cases we may have a sample that exhibits a pattern, and we may know of no cases violating that pattern, but we are not warranted in projecting that observed pattern onto all cases. To do so may in specific cases constitute the fallacy of hasty generalization (discussed in the chapter on informal fallacies). Yet in other cases we may have a sample that exhibits a pattern, we may know of no cases violating that pattern, and we may be thoroughly justified in projecting that observed pattern to all similar cases. Recall Andrea's argument. Melissa was indeed making a serious mistake—logically and financially—in not accepting that argument.

What distinguishes those two types of cases? What makes inductive arguments weak or strong? Under what conditions is it logically proper to generalize from a limited number of cases of some type to all cases of that type? In general, an inductive inference is good when the sample is representative of the entire species, and not so good when the sample is not representative of the species. (Here the term *species* refers to an entire type; in logic it is not a specifically biological term). The problem is that we typically do not know in advance whether the sample is representative or not. To know that would be to know that the pattern we've identified in the sample is indeed exhibited in the entire species. But that's exactly what we're trying to make an inductive case for—that the identified sample pattern does in fact hold generally! Are there steps, then, we can take that give us a better chance of getting a representative sample, or that make it more reasonable to *believe* that we have a representative sample, so that we can legitimately conclude that the familiar pattern is indeed a general one?

There are three important considerations concerning the samples on which inductive arguments are based:

IIIA. EXISTENCE OF THE IDENTIFIED PATTERN

The first requirement is that the pattern you claim to see in the sample really must be in the sample. Recall that Andrea insists that *everyone* on the planet is aware of the specific sort of scam. Melissa counters that Andrea is *always* harsh and judgmental, and that she is *always* harping about evidence. Neither of those claims is actually true, of course. In each case, a characteristic observed in *some*—perhaps even many—cases has been elevated to an alleged universal pattern. If you've read the chapter on informal fallacies, you may have already recognized such claims as hasty generalizations.

IIIB. APPROPRIATE SAMPLE SIZE

The smaller the sample, the easier it is to find patterns exhibited within it. And that is a problem, because many of those patterns will be a mere coincidence without real significance. Projecting them onto all similar cases will almost inevitably lead to false conclusions. Suppose that for some strange reason you have encountered only two dogs in your life. It might well be that all the dogs in your sample are brown, loud, slobbery, prone to rolling in, well, whatever, and very affectionate. But as your sample grows, most of those "patterns" will quickly disappear. By the time you have met 15 dogs, it is likely that almost none of those patterns any longer characterizes your updated sample of dogs. Your expanded sample has become a little more representative, since none of those initial patterns in fact characterize all dogs. So simply increasing the sample size is one way to raise the likelihood that the sample from which you are inductively generalizing is representative of all similar cases.

But here two cautions must be noted.

First caution. Even having a huge sample does not guarantee that it is representative. Until fairly recently, medical research was notorious for conducting studies largely on males, then generalizing the results to all humans. Males are indeed human (for the most part), and over decades studies have been conducted on millions of them. So the sample size was huge. But the sample was nonetheless defective. It was unrepresentative of humans as a whole because it systematically overlooked roughly half of them, a half that was in important ways physiologically different from the half studied. That oversight seriously skewed the sample and resulted in some badly mistaken inductive generalizations. The result was that for decades women were subjected to a number of medical treatments that were appropriate for men with certain conditions, but not at all for women with the same conditions. Here, induction on a skewed sample had serious practical consequences. This is another case where getting some particular piece of logic right is vitally important.

Second caution. On the other hand, a large sample is not always necessary. In some cases it can be reasonable to believe that even a relatively small sample is representative of the whole species in question. For instance, as we noted earlier, science has examined a vanishingly small fraction of the electrons in the cosmos (past, present, and future)—very nearly 0% of them. Yet science confidently pronounces on the mass and charge of *all* electrons everywhere and always. The same holds for all cows having four stomachs, all copper conducting electricity, and on and on. Can those general conclusions based on such a small sample really be legitimate?

As it turns out, this issue is extremely complicated. But we'll see later in the chapter on scientific inference that science operates with a number of presuppositions—a crucial one being the *principle of the uniformity of nature*. Scientists thus take it that nature makes all electrons just alike and makes electrons unique and distinct from every other type of thing— from protons, neutrons, brussels sprouts, and musk oxen, to name a few. Electrons, on this view, constitute a category, a type, a species of genuinely real, separate things with their own identity, characteristics, and patterns. They are something that nature itself "recognizes"—a **natural kind**, as they are often called. If that is correct (and again, these issues are complicated), then key defining patterns exhibited within even small samples of electrons, copper, and cows will indeed be representative of defining patterns among all electrons, all copper, and all cows. So relax. Science is not built upon layer upon layer of hasty generalizations.

IIIc. APPROPRIATE SAMPLE SELECTION

As noted above, samples can be unrepresentative even if they are enormous. But if a sample is widely diversified, it is less likely to be skewed in one direction to the exclusion of others, more likely to be broadly representative. Imagine the differences in results of election predictions based on political polls taken within samples composed exclusively of

- members of private golf clubs; or
- patients at a free inner city medical clinic; or
- shoppers at a suburban mall.

Focusing on any one of those groups would not produce very accurate election predictions. But a diverse sample involving carefully chosen proportions of all three (plus many other groups) is likely to provide a much more representative sample, allowing for much stronger inductive arguments—and much more accurate predictions. Sampling techniques have gotten so sophisticated and precise that national professional polling organizations can generate surprisingly accurate results after polling as few as 1,000 people in the US—about 1/3000 of 1% of the entire population. Again, small size is perfectly OK when the sample is fairly representative. There is no absolute guarantee that a broadly diverse sample will be representative, but the chances are certainly improved.

IV. Summary and Conclusion

Inductive arguments involve taking a familiar pattern found in cases of some type and projecting that pattern on a present case of that type, future cases of that type, or all cases of that type. It is a very common sort of inference. It is also an inference that can easily go wrong. In fact, it is one of the very few types of inference so frequently misused that the misuse has its own special name—the hasty generalization. As the medical research case involving males and females mentioned above makes clear, important everyday matters—matters as important as proper health care, even life and death—sometimes depend upon the quality of our inductions. Many far-reaching scientific theories also depend upon inductive generalizations and the presuppositions that underlie them. Even ordinary everyday matters—thousands of them—depend upon our implicit inductive reasoning. As with other areas of logic we've discussed, getting the logic right can be crucial.

This is a lesson that Melissa learned the hard way. (And after what happened, she would be so very grateful for any help you could give her on next semester's tuition. If you will just e-mail her your account information, plus the PIN or password, she will be happy to take care of the rest of the details.)

V. Addendum: The Problem of Induction

In practical life we cannot avoid using induction in even the most ordinary of everyday matters. We think about and understand things against the background of familiar patterns in nature—patterns whose future continuation we anticipate in our behavior at each moment going forward and in our plans for the future. Our inductive reasoning rests upon the assumption that the cases we encounter in the future will exhibit the same pattern we have seen in the past, or, again, that the future will be like the past in the specified respects. Without this assumption we'd sit down to our umpteenth bowl of cornflakes and say to ourselves: I have no idea what will happen when I eat this cereal. Maybe I'll be nourished. Maybe I'll burst into flames. Maybe I'll be appeared to by Spiderman or turn into an aquarium. We wouldn't know what to think. Experience to date would be entirely uninstructive.

As noted earlier, science presupposes that the fundamental patterns of physical reality do not change arbitrarily and randomly. Without that presupposition, it is not clear how science could attempt to make sense of nature. Science searches for the regularities within nature. So science presupposes (indeed, it must presuppose) that the deep principles of nature are stable. In large part, science just is a careful, rigorous effort to identify those stable patterns, and to understand those patterns by finding underlying explanations for them. Within science the presupposition of pattern stability is referred to as the principle of the uniformity of nature.

So it appears that across the entire spectrum of human thinking we cannot help but place implicit faith in this underlying inductive principle: that the patterns we encounter in the future will resemble the patterns that have persisted unbroken in the past, in short, that the future will resemble the past.

But here David Hume raised a difficult question. Granted, we unavoidably assume and employ the inductive principle. But do we have any good reason for thinking that the principle is true? If we don't have good grounds for it but still use it anyway, are we being irrational? Could science itself—which many see as the pinnacle of rationality—actually be irrational? Surely not, it would seem. So then how do we defend the inductive principle?

Here's where the rubber hits the fan. It looks to many philosophers as though we have only three rational options:

The principle that the future will be like the past

- is a necessary truth;
- can be established by deduction from the observed patterns of reality;
- can be established by induction from the observed patterns of reality.

The problem is that none of the three options works. None comes even close. Let's consider them in turn.

Necessity. We do not expect nature suddenly to abandon old patterns of behavior and begin exhibiting new ones; we don't expect the rules of gravity to change, for instance. But *could* nature do that? Think of it this way: could God at any point change the patterns of nature if God so chose? Clearly, the answer is yes. That means that the inductive principle is not a necessary truth. Logically speaking, established patterns can change—the future does not have to be like the past in the relevant respects.

Deduction. Since the patterns can in principle change, it would be possible for the past to exhibit one set of patterns while the future exhibits an entirely different set of patterns. Given the definition of validity discussed in the chapter on deduction, that means that the stability of nature's patterns in the past does not deductively imply that the same patterns will continue. So deduction thus isn't the answer either.

Induction. Wouldn't the unbroken uniformity of past patterns in nature at least give us a very good basis for inferring inductively that those long-observed, long-confirmed past natural patterns are likely continue?

Here Hume throws us a nasty curveball. Don't be surprised if you swing and miss the first few times you try to hit it.

How would we go about trying to establish *inductively* that nature's patterns won't change, that the future will be like the past in the relevant respects? Well, we would construct an inductive argument based on the stability of relevant patterns in the past, and conclude on the basis of that past stability that it was probable that those patterns would continue in the future. Inductive arguments do indeed begin from patterns in the past, but, as we've seen, in moving to a conclusion about the future they implicitly employ the underlying inductive assumption that the future will be like the past in the relevant respects. The problem here is that the underlying inductive assumption upon which our argument depends is the conclusion that the argument is supposed to establish. In short, any attempt to establish the inductive principle by induction will assume the very principle it wants to establish. This is a clear case of the fallacy of begging the question (discussed in the chapter on informal fallacies).

This is Hume's **problem of induction**: there is simply no way to avoid using inductive inferences. For induction to be rationally legitimate, its fundamental underlying principle must be rationally legitimate. But of the three standard possible ways of rationally justifying that underlying inductive principle, the first is a falsehood (it is *not* a necessary truth), the second a deductive failure (it is *not* deductively valid), and the third is blatantly circular (it *assumes* the inductive principle, which is exactly what's at issue).

The problem of induction has proven to be a very difficult philosophical puzzle. Various solutions have been proposed by the likes of Thomas Reid (1710–1796) and Immanuel Kant (1724–1804), among others. Whether any these proposed solutions represent real progress remains controversial. But regardless of our philosophical position on this topic, we humans can't manage long without inductive reasoning, be it conscious or unconscious; and we will manage better if our inductive reasoning is good.

7.

Mill's Methods

"No way," declared Melissa. "I don't do needles."

"Oh really?" Andrea responded. "What about the tattoo you got on your . . ."

"All right, all right. Don't remind me. But that was different. I didn't even know I had gotten it until the next morning when I was getting ready to take a shower. But the point is, shots can cause all sorts of nasty things. Remember a few years ago when flu shots were causing some weird disease? And lots of people think that some vaccines can cause autism in kids." Andrea merely snorted sarcastically at that claim. "Even when you get a simple tetanus shot, they make you read a pretty scary warning about the possible side effects. Anyway, I am not getting any HPV shot."

"Look, it doesn't seem to cause any serious side effects. All it does is make your immune system produce some antibodies that keep you from getting the virus that in some cases can lead to cervical cancer—which is a really, really horrible disease."

"Of course," René chimed in, a bit smugly, "anyone who is chaste doesn't have to worry about that virus."

"Oh come on, René, you're always blaming the victim. And just for the record, Melissa, you've got a way better chance of tattoo needles giving you hepatitis C than a flu shot or HPV shot causing some weird problem."

I. Reasoning about Causes

In the conversation above, the idea of causation comes up quite a few times. And that's not unusual. Beliefs about causation pervade our thinking, reasoning, conversations, decisions, and behavior. Our conception of reality includes the idea that reality has specific causal structures. Our choices are frequently made in light of what we think the causal effects of certain actions will be. Our assessments of moral responsibility often depend on the causal consequences of our choices and behavior, and on whether we knew or should have known what those causal consequences would be. Beyond that, we take the events in nature itself to be deeply intertwined with the patterns, principles, and laws of cause and effect. Causation seems so pervasive that some thinkers argue that absolutely everything—including our deepest inner thoughts, feelings, beliefs, decisions, and actions—are caused by things and forces outside of us.

Disputes over cause and effect relationships characterize political and policy debates as well. In the recent past there have been hot disputes over whether human activity caused global warming; whether the HIV virus caused AIDS; whether violent movies, videos, and music caused violent behavior; whether greed caused the financial crash of 2008; whether cell phone use caused cancer; whether having an abortion caused depression. Some of those issues have been settled. But new questions continually arise: Do full-body airport scanners have dangerous health effects? Do GMOs cause environmental problems? Will the president's policies create huge economic problems?

Identifying specific causes and their effects is often difficult and controversial. The patterns of cause and effect are often complex, and the multitude of factors involved in a situation often make it hard to tell what is cause, what is effect, what is causally relevant, and what is a matter of sheer coincidence. Your dog barks at a passing stranger; five minutes later you get a headache—most likely a mere coincidence, but maybe not. Sometimes two things occur together with a high degree of frequency; they are strongly correlated. We suspect that there is a causal relationship between the two. But the causal relationship—the arrow of causality—could go either way. Suppose researchers establish a strong correlation between obesity and depression. It may be the case that obesity causes depression: given our culture's obsession with thinness, no wonder obese people tend to be depressed. Or maybe depression causes obesity: depressed people eat more because they find emotional comfort in food. A third possibility is that neither obesity nor depression is the cause of the other, but that they are both caused by a third factor. Maybe a hidden hormonal imbalance causes both hunger and depression. Or maybe, in the end, the correlation was accidental, and there is no causation to be found here at all.

So reasoning about causes can be tricky. "Correlation is no guarantee of causation" —so goes the standard caution here. Nonetheless, in our day-to-day lives we unavoidably take ourselves to be dealing with causes and effects on a continual basis, and our beliefs and actions frequently depend upon reasoning about causes and their effects. As we've seen with other types of reasoning, causal reasoning often transpires on an unconscious level. It's virtually automatic. Even when a situation requires deliberate causal reasoning, that reasoning is often quite intuitive, natural, and straightforward.

Here's an example we can easily imagine happening in ordinary life. Suppose that you come down with apparent food poisoning. You immediately wonder what you have eaten that might have caused it. You haven't eaten off campus all week, and you have eaten only your usual food service favorites, except that yesterday you picked up a California roll from the food service sushi bar, which you rarely do. Maybe that was the cause. It's at least a reasonable first suspect. Then you find out that there are 14 other cases of apparent food poisoning on campus, and it turns out that every one involved California rolls. That information makes you more confident in your original suspicion. One more fact emerges. You only had one roll, and your case is fairly mild. But several people had two of them, and two people even had three—and the more rolls people had the sicker they got. Case pretty much closed: it was the California rolls.

Your reasoning was perfectly natural. There was nothing tricky or out of the ordinary about it. And your reasoning was good. You in fact engaged in at least three classic types of causal reasoning, three of five modes of causal reasoning known as **Mill's methods**, named after the British philosopher John Stuart Mill (1806–1873). His methods capture some basic ways of thinking about relatively simple cases involving causation. Mill did not invent these techniques of reasoning. People make use of them all the time without philosophical instruction. But he tried to identify them and delineate their structure so that by consciously and intentionally employing them we could think through issues of cause and effect more rigorously, more methodically, and more accurately. The methods are aimed at helping us to identify the cause or causes in specific cases and to separate them from other factors. The methods embody five perfectly natural ways of thinking, so natural that in the food poisoning case you employed three of them without even being aware that they are methods of causal reasoning.

II. Mill's Methods

IIA. THE METHOD OF DIFFERENCE

You and your friends go out for pizza. You order three large pizzas.

- Pizza One has Anchovies, Green Peppers, and Mushrooms (A, G, M).
- Pizza Two has Mushrooms, Green Peppers, and Sausage (M, G, S).
- Pizza Three has Olives, Pepperoni, and Mushrooms (O, P, M).

After the meal, two members of your group, Andrew and Ian, get violently ill. You suspect food poisoning. But which food item was the culprit? You review what each of you ate. Andrew had pieces from Pizza One and Two, Ian from Pizza One and Three. The others just had pieces from Pizzas Two and Three.

- Andrew and Ian had ingredients A, G, M, S, O, P. Event occurs
- The others had ingredients G, M, S, O, P. Event does not occur

The others did not get sick. So it appears that Green Peppers, Mushrooms, Sausage, Olives, and Pepperoni were not the source of the problem. What did Andrew and Ian have that the others did not? The Anchovies. It is most likely, then, that Anchovies are the culprit.

J. S. Mill calls this method of reasoning about causes the *Method of Difference*. Here one is searching for the unique element in the antecedents of an event, one thing that shows up when an event occurs, but does not show up when an event does not occur. In this case the event was an illness of the food poisoning sort, and the unique antecedent, as far as we can tell, was Anchovies.

IIB. The Method of Agreement

Let's change the example. Same pizzas, but this time everyone get sick except Ian. As before, Andrew ate pieces from Pizza One and Two; others ate from Pizzas One and Three, and Two and Three. But Ian restricted himself to Pizza Three. So what element did those who got sick share in common?

- Andrew: A, G, M, S   Event occurs
- Others (1, 3):   A, G, M, O, P   Event occurs
- Others (2, 3):   G, M, S, O, P   Event occurs

This narrows the list of possible culprits down to two: Mushrooms and Green Peppers. They are the only elements that show up in all cases where people got sick.

J. S. Mill calls this the *Method of Agreement*: you look for the common element where the event occurs. If you're lucky, there will be only one element. But we have two. Can we narrow the list of two possible culprits down to one? For that, we turn to another strategy Mill identified.

IIC. The Joint Method of Agreement and Difference

We work with the same scenario as above, but add Ian in.

- Andrew (1, 2):   A, G, M   Event occurs
- Others (1, 3):   M, G, S   Event occurs
- Others (2, 3):   M, G, S, O, F   Event occurs
- Ian (3):   O, P, M   Event does not occur

Now we ask ourselves, of the two shared elements that the others ate, which one shows up on Ian's list? He ate it and did not get sick. So that would eliminate it as a causal factor in the case of food poisoning. The element that gets off the hook is Mushrooms. Green Peppers and Mushrooms show up as a common element for all who got sick, but Mushrooms show up on a list for a person who did not get sick, while Green Peppers do not show up on that list. That leaves Green Peppers as the likely guilty party. The *Joint Method of Agreement and Disagreement* narrowed the list down to one. Here we are looking for a common element that is present when the event occurs but absent when the event does not occur.

IID. THE METHOD OF CONCOMITANT VARIATION

There are a couple other methods for identifying a probable causal factor. One of them is the *Method of Concomitant Variation*. Consider the following case: Katrina gets sick after almost every meal. We suspect a food allergy of some sort. But she eats all sorts of food. After tracking her food intake for several weeks, we notice that the more milk (or milk products) she has, the sicker she gets. The less milk she has, the better she feels. And when she has no milk, she has no symptoms as all. The same is not the case for meat, vegetables, fruit, nuts, eggs or berries. So we rightly suspect that milk is the problem, that Katrina is lactose intolerant. Of course, we could be wrong. It's an outside possibility that a hidden third factor is involved, that a strange chemical imbalance causes her both to crave milk and to feel sick. But at least we're on the right track. Generally, the method of concomitant variation looks for factors that vary together on a regular basis. One goes up, the other goes up; one goes down, the other goes down. Or, one goes down and the other goes up; one goes up, and the other goes down. An example of latter can be found in the connection between potassium levels and irregular heartbeat. When a person's potassium levels go down, the incidence of irregular heartbeat goes up. If that's your problem, your doctor might suggest you eat more bananas, which are potassium rich. If one of the factors precedes the other in time, then it is probably the cause of the other factor's variation. But if the two factors are simultaneous, we might need a causal theory that tells us which way the arrow of causality is pointing.

IIE. THE METHOD OF RESIDUES

This method is fairly simple, but we sometimes get it wrong. Grace, conscientious vegetarian that she is, goes to the Tree Hugger store to buy some bulk quinoa. She brings her own container. She puts several scoops of quinoa in the container and puts the container on the scale to find out how much quinoa she's buying. The scale reads 21 ounces. But what part of that weight is due to the quinoa and what part to the container? She doesn't want to pay for the container. She brought that in herself. Now she realizes she forgot to weigh the container first. So she dumps out the quinoa and weighs the container separately. It comes in at 3 ounces. She fills the container back up and weighs the whole package again. The scale reads 21 ounces once more. She knows the entire weight of the package is 21 ounces. That's the whole effect of the container and the quinoa. She knows that the container causes the 3-ounce part of that effect. So by subtracting 3 ounces from 21, she gets the cause of the remaining effect. The quinoa weighs 18 ounces. The cause she was looking for, the weight of the quinoa in the container, is left over (it's the residue) after the known cause of another part of the effect (the weight of the container) is subtracted.

Pretty straightforward. But we sometimes forget to do the subtraction when we are confronted by certain numbers. Say you hear a report that the national highway death toll over the Labor Day weekend in 2009 was 351. Wow, you say to yourself, the holiday traffic was really brutal that year—351 deaths. But what you need to do is subtract the average daily traffic death toll to find out what part of the effect was due to the holiday traffic. The average daily traffic death toll for 2009 was 102. That makes for a three-day average of 306. The holiday driving then accounts for 45 deaths. Still tragic, but less than one additional traffic fatality per state.

III. Summary and Conclusion

Our world is shot through with causal connections. And we care about a lot of them. We want to know what causes cancer, depression, bad weather, violence, poverty; we want to know what causes vibrant health, social harmony, strong economies, happy marriages, perfectly foamed milk for cappuccinos. But it's often difficult to know what causes what, difficult to sort out the tangled skein of causal factors in any particular case. J. S. Mill distinguished and described a number of useful methods for identifying causal factors. Those methods are used in everyday reasoning about causes, as well as in scientific research. Familiarity with these methods can help us be more systematic and more successful in identifying causes. In other chapters of this text we take up the related issues of explanation and scientific inference.

8.

Probability

René closed her eyes, took a big mouthful, made a horrible face and swallowed. And then shuddered.

"Why do you keep doing this to yourself?" Andrea asked—already knowing the answer.

"Because I need to lose 20 pounds—again—and this time keep it off. And according to the ads, for at least the first year this stuff gives you a 37% greater probability of keeping it off."

"37% greater than *what*? 37% of nothing is still nothing, you know. You're always looking for some magic weight control product, and they never work. Do you have any idea how much you've spent in the last year chasing thin?"

"Look—it isn't just vanity, and I'm not just letting myself be bullied by the fashion industry or cultural expectations. Or by anyone else's opinion for that matter. Like Keith's. Especially not Keith's, the rat. It's a health concern. You've seen the numbers about obesity—increased probability of heart problems, diabetes, and nearly everything else. I forget all the percentages, but my doctor is impressed by them anyway. Plus you know this thing with my knee from soccer—she said that I could lower the probability of further deterioration by 15 to 20% if I lost 20 pounds."

"That's fine. But I still want to know about this alleged 37%—aha! Here it is. Did you read the small print on this bottle? It only works, quote, "in conjunction with a program of continuing diet and ongoing exercise." Oh this is even better: "May increase risk of back spasms, and in a small percentage of users may lower immune response by up to 11%." So it looks like this stuff by itself does basically nothing—except, of course, raising the probability of other problems. At least, that's what it looks like depending on what all these probabilities are supposed to tell us—or maybe supposed to not tell us. They don't give you enough information to figure out what the numbers even mean or what they are supposed to be compared to. So like with most hyped cures, when you combine all the probabilities pro and con you can't tell what the real bottom line is."

"Nitpick all you like, Andrea, but I'll bet that this stuff improves *my* bottom line."

The conversation finally registered with Melissa, who had been texting some guy she had just met online about what she was going to do when she won the Mega Millions lottery. In a typically delayed reaction, she looked up at René: "Did you say 37%? Wow, that's impressive! I'm going to try it—where do you get it?"

I. Probability: Some Basic Concepts

In the foregoing conversation, references to probabilities are frequent, as are questions concerning exactly what information probabilities convey and what can be inferred from them. And like all of us, René has made some relatively important decisions on the basis of probabilities. Probabilistic thinking is a pervasive but often hidden factor in daily life. Insurance companies, stockbrokers, state lottery officials, casino bosses, health care facilities, cosmetic companies—all rely heavily on probabilistic inferences. People in businesses like these try to constrain events and control their outcomes as tightly as they can—often to their profit, of course. And they are pretty good at it. Soft drink companies can tell you (in the fine print) how outrageously poor are the odds of your winning any of their contests no matter how much of their product you buy. Casino bosses can virtually guarantee their backers a significant profit margin. And state lottery commissions can tell you (although they would really prefer not to) how massively overwhelming is the probability that your lottery ticket will be a dead loss.

Probabilities play key roles in intellectual disciplines as well: physics (radioactive decay, quantum mechanics), chemistry (gas laws, thermodynamics), biology (evolution, mutations), astronomy (multiverse theory, cosmological fine tuning), health care (prognoses, treatment choices, drug testing, epidemiology), and so on.

Probabilities also factor into many ethical decisions. For instance, moral questions of whether we should employ certain medical procedures in specific cases, whether it is appropriate to adopt certain laws, or whether we are permitted to follow a specific military strategy can often partially depend on whether doing so involves morally unacceptable high probabilities of specific harms, or on the comparative probabilities of producing favorable versus unfavorable outcomes. Indeed, some entire moral systems rest in part on the calculation of probabilities—for example, the likely outcomes of proposed actions, a fundamental consideration in classical utilitarian views, can be given probabilistic construals.

Even religious disputes sometimes have a probabilistic turn. Consider Pascal's Wager concerning the consequences of belief or disbelief in God. More recently intelligent-design advocates (and others) have argued that the probability of certain key life-supporting features of the physical cosmos occurring by chance is so prohibitively low (e.g., sometimes far less than 10^{-50} by their calculations) as to rule out chance as an explanation. The low probability, they argue, implies a designer.

Despite the pervasive importance of probabilities in various aspects of our lives, many of us do not have a firm grasp either upon the basics of probability or upon the ease with which we can stumble into faulty reasoning concerning probabilities. Fewer still are familiar with the inner workings of probability (axioms, theorems, definitions, derivations, inferences, foundations, interpretations, and so forth.). But given the pervasiveness of probability in our lives, the inescapability of basing decisions on probabilities, and the potential consequences of error in probabilistic reasoning, having at least some understanding of probability is important.

Although there are some subtle complexities when it comes to determining probabilities, in well-defined, "classical" cases with exactly specifiable, equally possible outcomes and boundaries (honest dice, fair coins, shuffled 52-card decks, thoroughly stirred balls in a lottery bin), precise odds and precise probabilistic calculations can be generated on the basis of mathematical considerations alone. For instance, a flipped coin can come down one of only two ways—heads or tails. If it is fair (making for an equal chance of either heads or tails), then since exactly 1 of those 2 equally likely ways is heads, there is a 1 in 2 chance of heads. That 1 in 2 chance translates into a probability of heads of 1/2, or 0.5. The same goes for tails. Or if the coin is two-headed, then there is only one possible result for any flip—heads. So the chances of getting heads is 1 chance in every 1 throw—1/1, or a probability of 1.0. And with a two-headed coin, there is no way whatever a flip can result in a tail, so there is a 0 chance in every single throw—every 1 throw—or 0/1 or 0.0 probability.

This is the classical way probabilities have been defined. Something that logically *has* to be true, or that is necessarily true (e.g., 2 + 2 being 4), has a probability of 1.0. Something that logically *cannot* be true, or that is necessarily false (e.g., someone simultaneously being both a bachelor and married), has a probability of 0. In between 0 and 1 is an infinite range of probabilities reflecting the proportion of chances of a specified outcome as a fraction of the total possible outcomes where all outcomes are equally possible.

II. Conditional Probability

Our belief that 2 + 2 equals 4 does not depend on any evidence outside the proposition itself—it is something we recognize to be true in and of itself. But in other cases we believe things on the basis of other things we believe. For instance, we believe that the accused is guilty because her fingerprints were on the broken glass. We believe that aspirin will help our headache because it has often done so in our past experience. The effect of such evidence is brought to bear on the probability of something being true via **conditional probabilities**—probabilities of something being true given the evidence in question. For instance (just picking some numbers for illustration), the probability that the tree outside your classroom will fall over today is pretty low—perhaps .001, one out of a thousand. (The probability is really much, much lower, but we can leave out a batch of zeros just for our discussion.) But the probability would surely be higher were there a 40 mph wind blowing—maybe .02, two out of a hundred. And if there were a 100 mph wind, the probability of the tree going over would be much higher still—say .6, six out of ten. The probability that the tree will fall over given the condition that there is a 40 mph wind blowing, and the probability that the tree will fall over given the condition that there is a 100 mph wind blowing would normally be displayed respectively as

$$\text{prob} \left[\frac{\text{the tree will fall over}}{\text{there is a 40 mph wind blowing}} \right] = .02$$

and

$$\text{prob} \left[\frac{\text{the tree will fall over}}{\text{there is a 100 mph wind blowing}} \right] = .6$$

More formally, a standard way of indicating that when we take into account specific given conditions (or evidence) E, the resulting probability of some event (or proposition or hypothesis) H is equal to x—i.e., that the probability of H being true given evidence E is the number x—is

prob $[H/E] = x$ (an alternative expression is prob$E$ $(H) = x$)

III. Conditional Probabilities and Arguments

We can now connect probability to some things learned earlier concerning arguments. Take an argument consisting of premises (P) and conclusion (C):

P_1 [premise]
P_2 [premise]
Therefore,
C [conclusion]

If the argument is deductively valid, (i.e. if the conclusion logically follows from the premises) and if all the premises are true, then the conclusion has to be true as well. Thus, for a deductively valid argument, it must be the case that the conclusion is true given the premises. But anything that *has* to be true has a probability of 1, as we saw earlier. Thus, if a proposition (C) *logically follows* from some other propositions (P), then the conditional probability will be

prob $[C/P] = 1$

But suppose that the argument is inductive. In inductive arguments the conclusion (C) does not follow with logical certainty from the premises (P), so the conditional probability will be

prob $[C/P] < 1$

Exactly how much less than 1 the probability might be depends upon the specific premises and conclusion, and that can lead to real difficulties determining exactly where on the probability scale various specific cases lie. Fortunately, probability theory offers some equations that can provide guidance in many cases. Some of the more basic equations can be found at the end of this chapter. Such equations (and a huge range of more complex equations and results) provide a degree of precision in many cases. But not in all cases, as we'll see shortly.

IV. Conditional Probability: Wider Applications

It's often easy to identify conditional probabilities of 1 and 0. But most things in life are not so neat and clear-cut. In everyday life we rarely deal with the rigidities of necessary truth or necessary falsehood, or with the trivialities of flipping fair coins or rolling fair dice, or with different possible outcomes all of which are equally likely. So, can probabilities be useful in real life? Even if probabilities could in principle be useful, in order to employ them we would need to be able to determine what the relevant probability numbers are. But most of the probabilities relevant to daily life fall somewhere in between 1 and 0—and there are zillions of fractions in that range. Can we nail down those probabilities with any precision?

In some cases it is relatively easy to determine exact probabilities between 1 and 0. For instance, with a fair die, there are exactly 6 possible outcomes for any roll, but exactly 1 way to get a two—so there is exactly a 1 in 6 (or .166) probability of rolling a two. The precise, determinable characteristics of the case dictate an exact .166 probability.

But other cases seem far more problematic. How on earth can we determine the actual probability—even given our various catalogs of evidence—of the tree outside your classroom being blown down today? Of intelligent life existing elsewhere in our galaxy? Of sea levels rising more than three feet in the next century? Of a particular medical procedure providing a cure in your own case? Of your being happily married in 20 years if you marry your high school sweetheart now? Of your having to live with your parents for more than 15 months after graduation? Most issues we deal with, like those just mentioned, are neither logical necessities nor logical impossibilities. And none of them seem to have a precise probability dictated by determinable characteristics of the cases. Even all of our evidence combined does not imply answers to such questions with any certainty, and although we may be able to narrow the range of the probabilities in some of these cases, in others the probability values would seem to be complete mysteries.

Furthermore, conditional probabilities will depend in part on what is accepted as given, on what background beliefs, evidence, and information are taken to be relevant to the issue in question (i.e., on the specific Qs in the conditional expression "prob [P/Q]"). And those things are often nearly impossible to settle to anyone's satisfaction, leaving us again with no way to pin down exact probabilities in particular cases.

V. Determining Probabilities

So who cares? Why should we even try to figure out such probabilities? At least two reasons are often given. First, as noted earlier, our lives daily depend on probabilities. Some things you do because you think that the probabilities of experiencing or causing harm are low (e.g., driving 5 mph over the speed limit on a country highway). Some things you refrain from doing because you think that the probabilities of experiencing or causing harm are higher (e.g., passing on a blind curve in the mountains). Some things you do trusting the judgment of other people who believe that the probabilities of your coming to harm are low: taking certain medications (trusting the drug testers), flying across the country (trusting FAA officials), having dental X-rays, using a cell phone, going through the scanner at a trendy clothing store, eating genetically modified foods, and on and on. Let's hope you're right in trusting the probability estimates of various people you've never heard of.

A second reason advanced by some is a claim that in order to be fully rational we must always proportion the strength of our beliefs to the strength of the evidence for them. On this view we should very firmly believe those things for which there is strong evidence, and put very little credence in ideas for which there is very weak or little evidence; where evidence falls somewhere between those two, we should adjust the strength of our beliefs accordingly. On this view, then, the degree to which we cling to a belief should reflect the degree to which the evidence makes it likely to be true. In other words, our beliefs should be adjusted to the conditional probabilities of those beliefs given the relevant evidence. On this view, believing something either more or less strongly than the degree to which the evidence makes it probable is a rational failure—even, according to some, a moral failure. To avoid such failures we have to know some at least rough probabilities. So again, how do we determine them?

In many cases we can collect empirical data concerning other instances of the type of case in question (as in inductive and analogical cases discussed elsewhere in this text.) We can generate statistics from data of past cases, and—done correctly—the numbers can provide some insight into probabilities in other cases. For example, take Florence Nightingale, well-known in the history of nursing but also the mathematically-trained inventor of the polar area diagram. She is generally credited with being the first person to collect empirical data and generate numbers that could be used medically. For instance, she was able to show that British soldiers in the Crimean War were seven times more likely to die of diseases than from enemy activity. This finding surprised many, as we can well imagine. But once her numbers forced reluctant officials to recognize the situation, Nightingale was enabled to address the causes of the high disease mortality. Probabilities were clearly life and death matters in this situation.

In many cases, however, the relevant evidence for determining conditional probabilities is buried more deeply. For instance, in trying to predict the future effects of climate change given certain levels of human greenhouse gas production, a great deal of theoretical modeling must be employed. And although the theoretical models have empirical bases, the data is more indirect and theoretically based than the data in medical testing cases or in Nightingale's Crimean War case. Thus the numbers for such conditional probabilities as

$$\text{prob} \left[\frac{\text{sea levels will rise } n \text{ feet}}{\text{greenhouse gases are produced at } m \text{ level}} \right] = x$$

may have real empirical connections but are harder to pin down precisely, generating bitter political disputes (but few competent scientific disputes) over whether the probabilities are high enough to warrant certain sorts of inconvenient actions. It is clear that scientific inferences and analogical reasoning—both discussed elsewhere in the text—will play roles here, but determining exactly how they factor into the probability calculation is difficult.

Things get even trickier in cases where there is virtually no hope of getting relevant data—even indirectly. For instance, what is the probability that in 250 years the state of Iowa will secede from the United States? What is the probability of continued global warming leading within the next few decades to armed skirmishes between Oregon and Nevada over water supplies? What is the probability that the first aliens to land on earth will be from the M81 galaxy?

Where do we even begin in such cases? It is not a logical certainty that we'll see alien visitors from M81, nor is it logically impossible—so the probability is somewhere between 0 and 1. But where? How do we find out? How do we even make intelligent guesses? We can't examine data concerning previous alien landings, and trying to construct theoretical bases for determining the probabilities here has only the most tenuous and controversial connection to either established theory or empirical data.

VI. Definitions and Disputes

But all is not completely hopeless. Even in the cases where precise probabilities are unattainable, we can sometimes determine comparative probabilities—that is, we can sometimes judge which of two possibilities is the more likely. Recall the example above of the falling tree. We might be unable to determine the precise conditional probabilities involving the 40 mph wind vs. the 100 mph wind. But even so, we can see pretty clearly that the probability of the tree going down in the 100 mph case is significantly higher than it is in the 40 mph case. And quite often that type of comparative probability, that ability to tell which of two probabilities is higher, is all we need in order to make sensible decisions.

Not surprisingly, at this point some disagreement arises. But surprisingly, the disagreement goes very deep. Much of it centers on just what probability even *means*—even what the basic concepts are. Historically, half a dozen or so different positions and proposals have divided mathematicians and philosophers. The **classical** interpretation involved precisely specifiable proportions of specific types of outcomes within limited sets of equally possible alternative outcomes. But among the other difficulties it may encounter, this view cannot handle messier cases where the range of possible outcomes is not conveniently limited and not all outcomes are equally likely—cases more true to life than the sort of cases that inspired this view, like the six equally likely outcomes of rolling a fair die. Others have argued for a **logicist** position, according to which probability is defined purely in terms of logical relationships (e.g., "partial entailment") within precisely defined systems. Unfortunately, no one has figured out how to reduce complex real-world cases into the sort of logical structures this view requires.

Much more popular is **frequentist** theory, according to which a probability is defined by the limit that the relative frequency of a specified outcome approaches within a sequence over the long run. For instance, to say that the probability of heads with a fair coin is .5 just means that as you keep flipping a fair coin indefinitely, the overall proportion of heads to total flips will get closer and closer to 1 out of 2, or ½. In cases that do involve strings of repeated or repeatable types of events—everything from rolls of dice to effects of medications to automobile accidents to lottery results to professional athletes voting Republican—frequentist views are typically what people have in mind when they think about probability. Indeed, that seems to be the default concept.

But many people argue that frequentist views can't be the whole story. Can we really know what is going to happen in a sequence in the long run—maybe involving zillions of events millions of years from now? And if probabilities are about patterns within sequences, can we sensibly talk about probabilities of single events? Or probabilities of unique events? What of the more puzzling cases mentioned earlier—M81 aliens and the like? In those cases there just aren't any repeated events. We can talk about the figures for how frequently 18-year-old males dent up their parents' cars, but as far as we know there haven't been any past alien invasions of the earth—from M81 or anywhere else. So talking about frequencies does not seem to help much in these cases. What, then, can probability really mean?

One response has been a **propensity** view, according to which probability is a measure of an actual property that individual things or events have. For instance, probability would be a measure of a property individual coins have, as opposed to a measure of runs or collections of flips of coins. On this view, the coin we flip itself has a physical property in virtue of which the probability of flipping a head is ½. That property in this individual coin, or this individual toss event, explains why flipping it forever would generate a frequency limit of ½. If there is such a property—such a propensity—then we could perhaps determine probabilities through scientific examination of this coin alone (or this unique event alone). We would not have to wonder what might happen if we flipped it forever, which we cannot do anyway. But this interpretation also faces some challenges. Among them: Exactly what sort of thing is a propensity? How might we identify one, or determine what specific propensities might mean for individual probabilities? Where do we look to find the relevant propensity in the M81 case? As you can imagine, battles among professionals rage.

One other position currently popular among philosophers (as well as some scientists and mathematicians) is a **subjectivist** interpretation of probability. Contemporary subjectivists link the probabilities of propositions to the strength of personal belief in, or the degree of confidence in, those propositions. This position is often called **Bayesianism** (or subjective Bayesianism) because of the prominent role it gives to Bayes' Theorem—a theorem of the formal mathematics of probability named after the Rev. Thomas Bayes, an 18th-century clergyman/mathematician. (The term "Bayesianism" used in this way is a bit misleading, since **Bayes' Theorem** is also endorsed by various nonsubjectivists as well.)

"Personal belief" may sound like an "anything goes" position. In some cases there are indeed wide divergences of belief among perfectly rational people—especially where empirical and theoretical connections are tenuous. For instance, there are competent, rational astronomers who believe that the probability of life elsewhere in the universe is very nearly 1.0, given the phenomenal size, age, variety, and number of galaxies in the universe. Other equally competent, equally rational astronomers believe that the probability of life elsewhere in the universe is very nearly 0.0, given the incredibly special conditions required for life to arise. Although there have been attempts to provide the estimates with firmer empirical foundations (e.g., the Drake Equation), obviously there is still a lot of room for different probability beliefs.

The 17th-century mathematician/philosopher Blaise Pascal and his friend Pierre de Fermat are credited with bringing mathematical rigor into thinking about odds, chances, and likelihoods. But then wouldn't a subjectivist Bayesian interpretation of probability be a huge step backwards? Bayesian subjectivists do not think so, although the reasons are a bit complicated. One major advantage those advocates claim is that subjectivism makes it possible to assign at least some sort of probability value in problematic cases like those mentioned earlier. Most of us would simply find that we don't have a very strong conviction that the first aliens to land here will be from the M81 galaxy. Since Bayesian subjectivists equate degrees or strengths of belief with probabilities, our extremely low degree of belief would translate into an extremely low probability assignment—in the M81 case, say, .000000001. Thus, subjectivism provides us with a specific probability (or probability range) in this case, whereas other views don't seem to have any good way to handle these sorts of cases at all.

But how does the subjectivist suggestion help? Isn't the proposed .000000001 probability in the M81 case just a wild guess, purely subjective and arbitrary? OK—so we've put a number on it. But not only is there no objective ground for that number, someone else who has an inexplicable fondness for M81 might have a much stronger belief here and might give the M81 case a probability millions of times higher, say,

.3. Aren't we still left with a free-for-all of opinions? Can't anyone say anything they wish when it comes to probabilities?

Not quite. Bayesian subjectivist probability does not allow one to believe just anything one wishes concerning probabilities. Subjectivists typically impose some fairly strict constraints on probability and beliefs. For instance, in order to be rational, one's beliefs and probability assignments must be internally consistent, consistent with the mathematics of probability (the standard axioms and equations of probability), and flexible in the sense that any new relevant evidence that arises must be taken into account. That means that relevant evidence cannot be ignored—*all* new relevant evidence must be recognized, and one's beliefs must be adjusted in order to accommodate the new evidence. In addition, the way new evidence is incorporated into one's beliefs, the impact that new data has on old beliefs, is not a matter of arbitrary personal choice. The specific way the strength of one's beliefs is adjusted to any new evidence must be governed by Bayes' Theorem (equation 11 in section IX of this chapter, an important mathematical consequence of the probability axioms concerning changes in conditional probabilities when the givens change, when new evidence arises). One might not like it that old beliefs are forced to change in response to new evidence, but that dislike is of no more relevance to the requirements of rationality than one's profound dislike for the mathematical requirement that if one misses 40% on an exam, 100% minus 40% leaves only 60% credit.

It is here that Bayesians see the real genius of their view. Suppose that two people have very different initial ideas about the probability of something—say, global warming. Suppose further that as new information comes in,

1. both people accept the data, whatever the data are, pro or con; and
2. both people continually adjust their initial probabilities in accord with Bayes' Theorem.

Under those conditions, it can be shown mathematically that no matter how far apart the two subjective probability assignments were initially (so long as neither is 1.0 or 0.0), over time the adjusted probabilities will come closer and closer together converging toward the same range.

So Bayesians will cheerfully admit that the initial subjective probabilities that two people hold may be far apart. At the outset, it may look like an arbitrary, subjective free-for-all. But, they argue, their Bayesian subjectivist view is superior in two important ways: first, it at least gives them initial values from which to start; and second, no matter where between 0 and 1 various people start from, as the data come in, the process of applying Bayes' Theorem repeatedly over time will lead to a convergence toward a more precise probability. Nonetheless, conceptual and practical disputes concerning probability are far from being resolved within the mathematical and philosophical communities.

VII. Fallacies and Cautions

Unfortunately, some of our basic intuitions about probabilities are not very reliable. Despite the fact that an enormous number of our actions, decisions, and beliefs depend in part on our perceptions of probabilities, we really aren't very good at recognizing or assessing a lot of the probabilities related to living in the contemporary world.

Just for fun, let's begin by exploring some of your probability intuitions. Without peeking ahead, write down your best guess at each of the following:

1. How many students would have to be in your class for there to be at least a .5 probability (a 50% chance) of two of those students sharing a birthday?
2. If you flip a fair coin 100 times, what is the probability that you will get exactly 50 heads and exactly 50 tails?
3. Which of these sequences of heads and tails is most probable if you are flipping a fair coin:
   a. T T T T T T T T T
   b. H H T H T H T T H T
   c. H H H T H H H H H T
   d. H H H H H H H H H H
4. If you are driving to a store to buy a ticket for a Powerball lottery, how far would you have to drive before the probability of your being killed in an automobile accident is greater than the probability of the ticket you buy being the winner?
5. How many times greater are the odds of your being killed by a terrorist while traveling abroad than the odds of your winning the Mega Millions lottery?
6. How many times greater are the odds of your being killed by a terrorist while traveling abroad than the odds of your dying

from falling out of bed or falling over a piece of furniture?

7. True or false. Your college's star soccer player scores on average once each game. Since she has not scored at all during the previous three games, she's *way* overdue. It's a good bet she will score at least twice in today's game.

Now, here are the answers:

1. The probability of two people sharing a birthday will be slightly over .5 in any group of 23. In fact, in a group of 50 it will be nearly certain: .97.
2. About .08 (roughly 1 chance in 12).
3. The probabilities are identical.
4. If you drive roughly 6 blocks one way, your chances of being killed in an auto accident before you get back home are approximately equal to the chances of your ticket being the big winner. That does not mean that there is a large chance of your being killed in an accident in those 12 blocks. It means that the odds against your winning the lottery are gigantic.
5. About 300 times: the odds of your being killed by a terrorist while traveling abroad are about 1/650,000; the odds of your winning the Mega Millions lottery are about 1/176,000,000.
6. It isn't. Your lifetime odds of dying from a fall involving a bed or other furniture is about 100 times greater than the odds of dying via terrorist activity while traveling abroad.
7. False.

How did you do? Most people will have missed at least five or six. There are many factors underlying our confusions in this area. A brief discussion of a few of those factors follows. We will then turn attention to some specific probability fallacies.

VIIa. Intuitive Assessments

Indeterminacy/indefinability. There are situations where we not only do not have information we need to determine probabilities, but we also cannot in principle collect the information necessary for even a very broad assessment of the probabilities. These sorts of situations are in part what inspired subjectivist views of probability. In these cases, we don't have much to go on. We can't check our intuitions against reality. Where such cases are relevant to everyday decisions, we must simply take our best shot and hope. Worse, there are some things (some specific oscillating mathematical sequences, for instance) that do not have limiting frequencies, and in such cases it may not even make sense to talk about probabilities. Here again, our intuitions are left out in the cold.

In all these sorts of cases, it is difficult to know whether our probability intuitions are right or wrong. But there are other factors that skew our intuitions in ways that clearly lead us astray.

Blinded by the numbers. We sometimes get impressed by significant sounding numbers and fail to stop to think about what they really mean. Here's an example: According to recent headlines, the rate of complaints against United Airlines *doubled* last year over the previous year—a 100% increase. Indeed, some news headers cited the "surge" in complaints while others bemoaned the "leap." The conclusion that many people drew is that service on United is really going downhill fast; it might be a good idea to start flying some other airline that does not have such a dismal complaint record.

Well, maybe that's right. But exactly what was the rate of complaints against United? How bad was it really? What were the numbers behind the headlined figures? Had we pursued the issue further, we would have found out that a year ago there were around 2 complaints per 100,000 passengers, and this past year there were nearly 4 per 100,000. The rate did indeed nearly double—from around 2/1000 of 1 percent to around a bit less than 4/1000 of 1 percent. But that's not exactly the picture that words like "surge" and "leap" bring to mind. In fact, it would only take one additional crabby hung-over Melissa out of every 50,000 passengers to account for that increase. But doubling in a single year—now that sounds serious, that grabs our attention. Without checking the background information, however, we have no clue what the initially cited numbers really mean. Recall how impressed René and Melissa were by the 37% claim despite the fact, as Andrea pointed out, they had not been given enough information to know whether there was any real reason to be impressed.

Availability/salience. Recall the 9/11 terrorist attacks in NYC. The attacks were massive, lethal, visually stunning, and emotionally riveting. And the casualty count was horrific: nearly 3,000 people destroyed in a matter of minutes. We now tend to view the world through a filter colored by those events. We feel threatened. Yet more Americans are killed every year by falling televisions than have been killed since 9/11 by terrorists. Nonetheless, we remain vastly more aware of the threat of terrorism. We check people out before they board airplanes, but not before they walk out of the box store with a new TV.

A deadly assault of any type typically gets our attention more effectively than everyday events, regardless of how frequent the everyday events may be. Deadly assaults have more emotional impact on us; they tend to dominate our perceptions and expectations. We bring our three-topping take-out pizza back to our homes, then lock our doors for security while we eat them, despite the fact that Americans are many times more likely to die of obesity-related causes than home invasion assault.

Indeed, every year 40 times as many people die of obesity-related causes in the US as did in the 9/11 attacks. But even trivial attempts to address the obesity problem through legislation are met with howls of indignation. Every year, over 30,000 Americans die by guns; over 11,000 of those are Americans murdering other Americans. But that annual toll—four times the 9/11 number every single year—only gets national attention after mass-murder events.

Effects like this involve what psychologists refer to as *availability* (or sometimes *salience*). The idea is that an occurrence that is more recent, more out of the ordinary, more memorable, more personal, or more emotionally affecting will operate as a more dominant factor in one's background information for assessing probability than other, perhaps equally relevant, pieces of information. The result is a skewed perception and assessment of associated probabilities. The effect of availability clearly informs our intuitions concerning the threat level of terrorism. But it affects other intuitions as well. For example, people who know someone who has suffered or died of a specific disease tend to see the statistical threat of that disease as higher than those who do not have such experiences. Of course, in some instances there may be very good reason for heightened awareness in those cases. Nonetheless, the heightening effect of personal experience frequently produces a misperception of probabilities.

VIIb. Fallacious Probabilistic Reasoning

Our thinking about probability is no more immune to human frailty than other sorts of reasoning. Unfortunately, probabilistic fallacies are generally less obvious than ordinary logical fallacies. Of the many types of defective reasoning concerning probability, we will briefly discuss just three: one relatively straightforward, and two a bit more complicated.

The gambler's fallacy. This is probably the best known and the simplest of the common probabilistic fallacies. Suppose that you are flipping a fair coin and get heads 10 times in a row. Knowing that in a sequence of flips heads and tails tend to even out over time to roughly half heads and half tails (since the probability in each individual case is .5), we naturally begin to anticipate that the evening-out process *has* to start soon as the sequence of heads gets longer. Our anticipation that the next flip will come out tails begins to grow. The probability of tails on the next flip must be increasing, we think, in order for things to get back to normal. Tails—even several tails—are surely due.

But with a fair coin, the probability of each flip is completely independent of what happened in previous flips. If the coin is fair, the probability that the next flip will be a tail is still just .5, regardless of how many heads in a row there have been up to that point. To think (or anticipate, or, worse, to bet) otherwise is to commit the **gambler's fallacy**.

The idea that some result is "due" is often a tip-off that the gambler's fallacy is being committed. Listen to nearly any sports broadcast and you are likely to hear someone comment that some hitter is about due for a hit or a home run, that some point guard is about due to start hitting her three-point shots, that some driver is way overdue for a win, or that some tailback is about due to break a big run. All are good candidates for the gambler's fallacy.

The conjunction fallacy. This fallacy is a bit more complicated. But let's take a shot at it. Here's what we know about René: René is a serious, committed, intelligent, educated, conservative Christian, dedicated to helping the world's hungry and deeply supportive of mission efforts in the developing world.

Given that information, which of the following is more probable?

A. René works for an auto insurance company; or
B. René works for an auto insurance company and also teaches Sunday school in her church.

Commonsense intuitions here are strong and pretty uniform. This sort of case was famously discussed by Amos Tversky and Daniel

Kahneman, in the October 1983 issue of *Psychological Review*. In cases like these, they found that 85% of those surveyed select options like B as more probable than options like A. The problem is this: that ranking is mathematically impossible. It is a straightforward consequence of basic probability equations (equation 8 in section IX) that the probability of a conjunction of P and Q (where those two are independent) cannot be greater than the probability of either of P or Q by itself. We can think of it roughly this way:

1. Whenever the conjunction $P \wedge Q$ is true, P will also be true.

But the reverse is not the case. If P and Q are independent of each other, then even if P is true, there is still a chance that Q might not be. So there can be circumstances in which

2. P is true while the conjunction $P \wedge Q$ is false.

Given 1 and 2 (and leaving out a few technicalities), the probability of the conjunction of P and Q will always be less than the probability of P alone. And, of course, the same will hold for Q for exactly similar reasons. Thus, the probability of the conjunction being true can never be greater than the probability of either conjunct individually.

Notice that B above is a conjunction, while A is one of the conjuncts. But as we've just seen, the probability of a conjunction can never be greater than either conjunct. That means that the probability of B cannot be greater than A, no matter what our intuitions might tell us. To argue that a conjunction can have a greater probability than either or both of its conjuncts is thus to commit the **conjunction fallacy**.

The intuitive tug toward B is due to the fact that given what we know of René, it seems very likely that she teaches Sunday school, whereas what we know of her gives us no particular reason for thinking that she works for an auto insurance company. So the addition of the reference to teaching Sunday school makes most people feel that B is more likely than A. But, as it turns out, that is a piece of fallacious reasoning when it comes to probability.

The base rate fallacy. This one is even a bit trickier. But let's take a shot at it. Imagine (and this does take some imagining) that there is a $20,000 prize to be given this year for the best undergraduate philosophy term paper in the nation. The size of the award creates a lot of interest, and

10,000 entries have been submitted. Now as you may know, term paper plagiarism is a serious problem, and many colleges and universities have invested in software designed to identify plagiarism in student papers. The particular software employed by the contest sponsors is actually quite good. In fact, about 95% of papers containing plagiarism are flagged as such by the software. But the software is not perfect. It misses about 5% of the cheaters, and there are also occasional false positives. In fact, about 3% of the innocent papers it checks are mistakenly flagged as containing plagiarism. But the software gets 97% of innocent papers right.

Much to Bruno's misfortune, the paper he submitted for the contest was flagged by the software as plagiarized. Bruno naturally insists on his innocence. And perhaps he is innocent. After all, the software does occasionally make mistakes. But really, who is going to believe he's innocent? Given the software's 95% success rate in catching the guilty, and the low probability of its being wrong about innocence, the chances of Bruno's being innocent aren't very good.

Take a moment to think about this: the software nails 95% of the guilty; if you are guilty, 19 times out of 20 it's going to get you. It makes an incorrect guilty pronouncement in only 3% of all cases; it gets 97% of the innocent correct. If the software says the Bruno cheated, what is the probability that he is innocent as he insists? 1%? 2%? Pretty low, right?

Most people would infer that the chances of someone like Bruno being innocent are not very good and that he has some explaining to do. But it turns out that the inference is not quite right. Here's why. Suppose that in the current case, only 20 people actually submitted papers containing plagiarism. We can expect that the software will catch 19 of them and that only 1 of the actual culprits will escape detection.

But the software also says "guilty" in 3% of the cases where people are in fact innocent. In the case under consideration, there were only 20 plagiarists out of 10,000 entrants, leaving 9,980 innocents. But the software will mistakenly claim that 3% of them—299 people—are actually guilty. Those plus the 19 cheaters identified come to a total of 318 overall guilty verdicts from the software. And of those 319, only 19 are actually guilty. Thus, only about 6% of those pronounced guilty by the software are actually guilty. So the probability that Bruno is guilty on the say-so of the software is quite modest, only .06. The overwhelming probability is that he is innocent. In fact, if only one person in the entire contest cheated —leaving 9,999 innocent—the software would still flag the papers of 3%—300 people. Here the probability of a flagged paper involving plagiarism would be very tiny indeed: at least 299 of those 300 authors would be innocent.

Where did our intuitions go wrong? Initially, we see that the probability of someone being pronounced guilty if they really are guilty is quite high:

a. prob [Pronounced guilty / Actually guilty] = high (in this case, .95)

But we have a tendency to invert that into a belief that the probability of being *actually* guilty if one is *pronounced* guilty is thus also high:

b. prob [Actually guilty / Pronounced guilty] = high
    (perhaps also around .95)

But is the following true in general for propositions *P* and *Q*?

c. prob [*Q/P*] = prob [*P/Q*]

or that if prob [*Q/P*] is high, then prob [*P/Q*] also be high? The answer is definitely no. If you refer to either equation 10 or equation 11 in the section IX, you will see that (c) above will be true *only* if prob [*P*] alone and prob [*Q*] alone—the *base rates* of the two—are the same. To thus infer (b) from (a) (or vice versa) is to presuppose that prob [Pronounced guilty] and prob [Actually guilty] have the same or nearly the same value. But in cases such as Bruno's, that is manifestly false. Neglecting to factor in the relevant base rate is to commit the **base rate fallacy**.

Naturally, there are many more ways of going wrong concerning probabilities, but the three ever-so-plausible fallacies discussed above will perhaps serve as representative cautions.

VIII. Summary and Conclusion

Probabilities are intended as measures of how likely something is—the prospects of some event occurring or the chances that some proposition is true. Conditional probabilities specify that measure as it is shaped when we take into consideration certain background events (actual or potential) or certain propositions. In daily life we place our trust in reasoning about probabilities when we password protect our e-mail account, lock our front door, install a smoke detector in our kitchen, or check our tire pressure before going on a long trip. And we take risks assuming that the probabilities are too small to catch up with us when we speed through a yellow light, light up a cigarette, buy another sugary drink in the college coffee shop, get a tattoo, download a term paper from the internet, put off a mammogram, text while driving, or get involved electronically with strangers. In cases like these, most of us do not know what the relevant probabilities are. And even if we did know what they are, we may not know how to think correctly about them or how to factor them into our decisions and actions. Indeed, there is a very high probability that most of us—and not just René and Melissa—need some serious help here.

We have covered some of the major pitfalls in our implicit beliefs about probabilities in this chapter. But there is much more to probability theory, and there are entire semester-long courses devoted its exploration.

IX. Probability: Some Basic Equations

BASIC BOUNDARIES

1. Probabilities for all propositions range from 0 to 1:
   $0 \leq$ **prob** $[P] \leq 1$

2. If a proposition P is necessarily true (e.g., $2 + 2 = 4$), then:
   prob $[P] = 1$

3. If a proposition P is necessarily false (e.g., some people are both married and bachelors), then:
   prob $[P] = 0$

4. If a proposition P is neither necessarily true nor necessarily false (e.g., there are more than 400 trees on this campus), then prob $[P]$ is between 0 and 1:
   $0 <$ **prob** $[P] < 1$

NEGATIONS

5. If a proposition P has a probability of some number x, then the probability of its negation is $(1 - x)$:
   prob $[\sim P] = (1 - $ **prob** $[P])$

DISJUNCTIONS

6. If proposition *P* and proposition *Q* are mutually *exclusive* (i.e., *P* and *Q* cannot both be true simultaneously, as in "Norway will win the next Winter Olympics" and "Canada will win the next Winter Olympics"), then:

prob [*P* or *Q*] = (prob [*P*] + prob [*Q*])

7. If proposition *P* and proposition *Q* are *not* mutually exclusive (i.e., *P* and *Q* *can* both be true simultaneously, as in "Sam enjoys her philosophy class" and "Sam is vegan"), then:

prob [*P* or *Q*] = (prob [*P*] + prob [*Q*] − prob [both *P* and *Q*])

CONJUNCTIONS

8. If proposition *P* and proposition *Q* are *independent* (i.e., whether or not one of them is true has no effect on the probability of the other being true, for instance, the first roll of a die is a 5, and the second role is a 2; thus [prob (*P*) = prob (*P/Q*)], and similarly [prob (*Q*) = prob (*Q/P*)]), then:

prob [*P* and *Q*] = (prob [*P*] × prob [*Q*])

9. If proposition *P* and proposition *Q* are *not* independent (i.e., whether or not one of them is true does have an effect on the probability of the other being true, as in "Your parents both vote Republican" and "You vote Republican"), then:

prob [*P* and *Q*] = (prob [*P*] × prob [*Q/P*])
= (prob [*Q*] × prob [*P/Q*])

CONDITIONAL PROBABILITY EXPRESSIONS

10. Conditional probability: If *Q* is not a necessary falsehood (i.e., if prob [*Q*] ≠ 0), then:

$$\textbf{prob } [\textbf{\textit{P/Q}}] = \frac{\textbf{prob } [\textbf{\textit{P} and \textit{Q}}]}{\textbf{prob } [\textbf{\textit{Q}}]}$$

11. Bayes' Theorem (a very important consequence of basic probability axioms governing the degree to which new evidence

bears upon previous probabilities). Starting with the probability of P on its own, Bayes' Theorem gives us the probability of P after Q is taken into account (i.e., it indicates the *difference* the new evidence Q makes to the probability of P being true):

$$\text{prob } [P/Q] = \frac{(\text{prob } [Q/P] \times \text{prob } [P])}{\text{prob } [Q]}$$

9.

Analogical Arguments

"Where were you at dinner, Andrea? You look worse than death warmed over." Melissa was in one of her less diplomatic moods.

"Well, if I look worse than you did when you came dragging in at 6:30 this morning, then just shoot me. Actually, that's not such a bad idea. That would at least cure this miserable cold I've had for the last two days. And the headache."

"You weren't around at lunch, either," noted René. "What's up?"

"I was in the middle of my follow-up experiment and couldn't leave it. I had a couple bananas—that's all I could find in the primate lab. But the good news is, I think we were right. And this could be really big." Andrea couldn't keep a tinge of excitement out of her voice, and a bit of color crept back into her face. "Remember a while back I was telling you about how chimps in the wild eat the blossoms of this one particular flower —*T. gesneriana* to be precise—when they have colds, and that their colds almost immediately start improving? Well about six weeks ago Prof and I isolated this really interesting complex compound called Di-α-bromochlorinated pyrodine $J^4 \beta_7$ from those blossoms. We've been calling it 'di-alpha 7' for short. Since it's the only really unusual substance in the blossoms, I thought that it might be the key, and that if concentrated di-alpha 7 injections helped lab chimps with colds, we'd be onto something. Well, it does more than help. I injected them yesterday—that's why I was monitoring them so closely today—and it seems to have absolutely cured all but one of them, and it still really helped that one. Within 24 hours. It really does seem to work!"

"Wow! Are you serious? If you can cure colds you're going to be famous!"

"Not to mention rich! I'll be your financial assistant." Melissa was always ready to help a friend in need.

"Uh . . . thanks, Melissa, but we've still got lots more experiments and tests to run. But for now I think I'll just crawl into bed and die. I hope that you guys don't catch this thing. It is seriously miserable."

René gave Andrea a speculative look. "You scientists can be so completely clueless. Why don't you just give yourself a shot of Doctor Andrea's Magic Monkey Cure? I mean, come on—you're an evolutionist, right? If you believe that monkeys are your cousins and that this flower extract works on them, shouldn't you conclude that it will work for *your* cold too?"

Andrea stood with a stunned look on her face for about eight seconds. Then, without a word, she turned and left the room, running in the direction of the lab.

I. Analogical Arguments: The Basic Pattern

The very natural line of reasoning that led Andrea to think that a shot of di-alpha 7 might help her cold was an **analogical argument**. In simplest form the basic pattern of analogical arguments is as follows: one sees two things (or groups of things) as relevantly similar (or analogous) to each other in some important respects; one notes an important additional fact about one of those things or groups; then, in light of the strong similarity between the two in the specified respects, one concludes that the additional fact in question *probably* applies to the other thing or group as well.

More formally, the basic pattern goes like this:

1. Two things/groups, $[a_1, \ldots]$ and $[b_1, \ldots]$, are similar in that they all have characteristics $[P_1, \ldots]$.
2. The first thing/group, $[a_1, \ldots]$, also has the additional characteristics $[Q_1, \ldots]$.

So,

3. Probably, the second thing/group, $[b_1, \ldots]$, also has the additional characteristics $[Q_1, \ldots]$.

Virtually every analogical argument is an instance of this basic pattern. Here's how the pattern works in the lab example above. The conclusion that di-alpha 7 may well help human colds depends upon some relevant similarities (some mutually shared properties) between human physiology and chimp physiology. Given those similarities, the additional fact we saw in the chimp case—that in all or nearly all cases the cold disappears when di-alpha 7 is administered—is then inferentially transferred to the human case, making it probable that the same fact (the cold disappearing upon administering di-alpha 7) will also apply in human cases.

Probing the chimp case just a bit more deeply in her research, Andrea saw a significant uniformity: in nearly every instance of a thing both having the physiological properties in question and having a cold (all the experimental chimps, so far), being given di-alpha 7 has resulted in the cold being cured. If she did her research carefully enough, observed a well-selected, representative sample, then that uniformity isn't very likely to be just a coincidence. There is very likely some connection between having the physiological properties the chimps share and the additional fact concerning the effects of di-alpha 7. In short, it is probable that having the specific type of physiology (biochemistry, morphology, genes, and other physical characteristics in question) would naturally result in having any cold cured by di-alpha 7. If so, then Andrea—having the relevant sort of physiology—would likely find that di-alpha 7 was effective against her cold as well. That would be a very reasonable expectation.

The outline of the basic pattern of analogical arguments given above follows a schema developed by the logician Irving Copi. In the light of Andrea's research, we can give a slightly more detailed account of the underlying logical structure of analogical reasoning:

1. We have examined quite a number of things [$a_1, a_2, a_3, \ldots$] all having properties [$P_1, P_2, \ldots$].
2. All or most of those things [$a_1, a_2, a_3, \ldots$], when investigated, have also had property [$Q_1, \ldots$].

So,

3. Probably, there is some connection between the properties [$P_1, P_2, \ldots$] and property [$Q_1, \ldots$] (1, 2).

But,

4. The new case we are now considering [b_1] is *similar* to the familiar cases [$a_1, a_2, a_3, \ldots$] in that it shares the important properties [$P_1, P_2, \ldots$].

Thus,

5. Probably, the current case [b_1] will turn out to share the further property [$Q_1, \ldots$] as well (3, 4).

Why does the conclusion follow only *probably*? Why is Andrea only *likely* to find di-alpha 7 effective against her cold? Why does this analogical reasoning not constitute some sort of *proof*? In part, because despite strong similarities humans are not chimps—there are some differences important enough that you have probably never even considered dating or marrying a chimp, no matter how cuddly. So while the physiological similarities are substantial enough to justify inferring that it is likely that the di-alpha 7/cure connection discovered in chimps would hold in humans as well, given the differences, that connection is not absolutely *guaranteed* to hold in humans. Some of those differences might prevent that connection from holding in the human case or at least make the likelihood very modest. Thus, the inference is inductive rather than deductive. Direct experimentation on humans might be required before we could be sure what the effects of di-alpha 7 on humans with colds might be.

Even though such arguments provide something less than a proof, we employ analogical reasoning all the time. Indeed, it is one of the most basic and important kinds of human reasoning. Because deductive arguments are simply not available in the overwhelming majority of real-life situations we face, analogical arguments often are the best arguments we have for thinking about crucial everyday matters and many philosophical issues as well. Why think that your pet dog can feel pain? An analogical argument concerning animal consciousness. Why try out cosmetics on rabbits before giving them to humans? Analogical reasoning that what is safe if smeared on sensitive bunny rabbit eyes is safe for humans. Why perform medical experiments on lab animals prior to human application? An analogical argument: given the similarities between humans and lab animals, effects on the two will likely be similar. Why believe that other humans are conscious even though we cannot experience their consciousness directly? The analogical argument for other minds. Why accept various scientific results (e.g., theories concerning climate change, the deep past, distant parts of the universe)? Again, analogical arguments projecting patterns we see here and now to other parts of space and time. Why believe in God? The analogical argument from design is one good reason, some will say.

Analogical reasoning is common in ethical and legal matters as well. Here's an example of the former. The increasingly influential view that we have extensive ethical obligations to some nonhuman animals rests ultimately on the following analogical reasoning. Humans have the capacity to experience pain, fear, and distress. Those capacities are direct functions (or at least correlates) of specific types of neural structures. But many nonhuman animals have neural structures similar to those of humans, so—analogically—it is likely that they have similar capacities, that they too can experience degrees of pain, suffering, and distress. But an additional step is possible here. Our capacities, especially the capacity to suffer, imposes ethically relevant obligations upon others. At a minimum, they impose obligations to avoid needlessly causing human pain, suffering, and distress. Since, it is argued, those capacities in humans generate ethical obligations, it is reasonable to believe that similar capacities in nonhuman animals generate similar ethical obligations. Hence the ethical concern for animals born, raised, and slaughtered in some of the more brutal factory farms.

With respect to primates and most mammals, many people find such arguments convincing. But at the level of, say, amoebas there are no relevantly similar neural structures, and the capacities on which the relevant ethical obligations would rest are simply absent. The analogical case seems to fail here. But saying exactly where the relevant similarities begin to unravel is virtually impossible. What should we think about guppies? Starfish? Slugs? Mosquitoes? Members of Congress? Do moths have the requisite capacities? Do we have ethical obligations toward wasp larvae? In all of these cases there are many similarities to humans—life, shared genetic code, shared ancestry, and the like. But while those similarities may be important for other considerations, they do not seem to support the ethical concerns discussed here. The shared characteristics do not seem relevant to the ethical "quality of life" considerations. There just do not seem to be strong enough relevant similarities to support an analogical argument that establishes an ethical obligation concerning the quality of life of amoebas even if we had any clues as to what the quality of life for amoebas might involve.

Given that we rely on analogical reasoning in so many situations, it is fortunate that we humans are pretty good at it. If you offer your dog a new kind of dog food and after the first bite the dog dies in agony, you don't have to puzzle over whether you should taste the dog food to see what the problem might have been. Although we are not dogs, we are in many biological respects enough like dogs to think that what happened to the dog would probably happen to us if we ate the same thing. That's very sensible analogical reasoning. And we're so accomplished at it that such reasoning is often nearly instantaneous and unconscious.

II. Assessment

Since analogical arguments are nondeductive arguments, they can have varying degrees of strength. The support that the premises of an analogical argument give to the conclusion can be anywhere on the spectrum from strong to weak to irretrievably bogus. Obviously, we want to give more credence to the stronger arguments, less to the weaker. So how do we assess such arguments? What makes analogical arguments stronger or weaker?

Let's look at an example of a weak argument. Suppose that some health food advocates are currently recommending ant extract as a dietary supplement. Advocates note that ants have a variety of special abilities, such as the ability to carry many times their own weight. Something in the ants obviously supports those remarkable abilities. Extract of ground-up ants, advocates would have us believe, will no doubt contain whatever that something is. So we can expect it to have corresponding remarkable positive health effects in humans.

The advocates are clearly advancing an analogical argument, moving inferentially from ants to humans. Unfortunately, ground-ant extract doesn't seem to live up to its inferred promise. The remarkable characteristics of ants don't seem to transfer to humans. There are just too many disanalogies in this case. Perhaps that is fortunate after all. Depending upon exactly what additional properties ground-up ant extract is supposed to produce in humans, one might awake to the disconcerting discovery that one had developed antennae and an extra set of limbs.

What went wrong with the health food advocates' argument? A number of things, two of which are particularly important for present purposes. First, since ants don't eat the extract of ground-up ants, it is unlikely that the source of their amazing abilities is to be found in the extract of ground-up ants. So it is unlikely that there is a *connection* between what advocates are selling and remarkable abilities of ants. And, of course, their analogical argument—like any analogical argument—depends upon such a connection. Second, there isn't that much *similarity* between human physiology and ant physiology. Indeed, that's the reason why no one would really worry about developing antennae and extra limbs if they were to take this supplement. Even if there were in ants a connection between whatever the ant extract contains and their remarkable abilities, there is little reason to think that this connection would transfer to humans. All analogical arguments depend upon relevant similarities; those similarities form the basis for the transfer of the additional trait in question from one case to the other.

Good analogical arguments must meet two key criteria. First, there must be a real connection between the properties noted and the additional characteristic in the known case; second, the known case and the case where we apply the additional characteristic must be similar in the relevant respects. More formally, using the abbreviations from the basic pattern stated earlier:

1. The *connection* between $[P_1, \ldots]$ and $[Q_1, \ldots]$ must be properly established in the $[a_1, \ldots]$ cases.
2. There must be relevant, sufficient *similarities* between the $[a_1, \ldots]$ cases and the $[b_1, \ldots]$ cases.

The ground-up ant extract argument fails on both those counts. We see no connection in ants between their remarkable abilities and the ingestion of ground-ant extract (since they don't ingest ground-ant extract); and there is very little physiological similarity between ants and humans. But even failure on one of these criteria is enough to undercut an analogical argument. Furthermore, connections can have different levels of strength, and similarities can come in varying degrees. Even partial failure under either criterion will weaken an entire analogical argument.

In the chimp lab example discussed earlier, Andrea did not learn that di-alpha 7 would have the effects it does on sick chimps simply by thinking about di-alpha 7 plus chimp physiology and then idly *inferring* that di-alpha 7 would have those effects on chimps. Had that connection between chimp physiology, medication and cure been something discoverable just by doing logic, just through an inference, researchers could have just called in a really good logician (such as one of your philosophy professors) and asked her simply to think about di-alpha 7 and chimps, and to reason out what effects would logically follow from giving it to the chimps. That would have saved researchers a lot of time, work, and money, not to mention saving the chimps a lot of stress, fear, and perhaps even pain. And it would have earned your philosophy professor a Nobel Prize in biochemistry. But oddly enough, Nobels in biochemistry are lamentably rare among philosophy professors. We must *discover* what experimental medications result in what effects through the painstaking work of empirical research. Knowing that in chimps specific chemicals and specific effects are indeed connected, we can then infer that it is likely that the same connection will hold in the case of humans. Humans have similar physiologies to chimps, and humans taking that medication will likely experience the same or similar effects. The logical strength and legitimacy of the inference from the chimp case to the human case, then, depends upon

1a. the *connection* between di-alpha 7 and a cure having been properly established in the chimp case; and

2a. humans being physiologically *similar* to chimps in the relevant respects and to a sufficient degree.

What factors are important in assessing the strength of connection and the degrees of similarity? With respect to the first criterion, properly establishing the connection involves multiple factors. It would be hard to give a complete list, but among the more important considerations are these:

- The more cases (e.g., the more chimps) involved the better.
- The more diversified the *type* of cases exhibiting the connection the better (e.g., if not just chimps but other primates or even, more diversely, cats, gerbils, etc., with colds were helped by di-alpha 7, the connection would be even more firmly established).
- The better prior independent empirical or conceptual reasons we have to think that the apparent connection is plausible and does not violate other principles we know, etc., the better.

Unfortunately, there are no hard and fast rules for how many cases are adequate to establish a connection, for how diverse the groups tested should be, for exactly what constitutes independent plausibility, and so forth. Human experience and judgment is often required, and in many cases there is some latitude for rational disagreement.

With respect to the second criterion, the specific sort of similarity involves the extent to which the two things or groups being compared share important characteristics, characteristics that may be relevant to the transferability of the connection. Here again, no complete list can be given. Indeed, what constitutes relevance is another matter in which there are no hard and fast rules. At least in the short run, human experience and judgment will play a role. Consequently, there's room for rational disagreement. In most cases there will be lots of similarities that are obviously irrelevant. In the di-alpha 7 case, the fact that chimps and humans are similar in having hairs in their ears and having jointed fingers, and do not hatch from eggs almost certainly has no relevance to effectiveness of specific treatments for colds. But the relevance or irrelevance of other similarities may be less clear. For instance, chimps and humans—unlike almost all other animals—are alike in their inability to synthesize vitamin C. Is that similarity relevant to the di-alpha 7 case? It might be nearly impossible to tell without more research, and there might well be disagreements about that. And such disagreements can get quite bitter in some cases—for instance, whether certain similarities between humans and various lab animals are of strong enough relevance to support inferences that worrisome side effects of specific food additives on those animals are likely to show up in humans as well. Whatever disagreements may arise in specific cases, there is nonetheless substantial agreement on two key factors that go into isolating relevant similarities:

- The similarities (analogies) between the $[a_1, \ldots]$ cases and the $[b_1, \ldots]$ cases are of a type and depth that support the inferential transfer of the connection from the $[a_1, \ldots]$ cases and the $[b_1, \ldots]$ cases.
- There are no significant differences (disanalogies) between the $[a_1, \ldots]$ cases and the $[b_1, \ldots]$ cases of a type and depth that might undercut the transfer of connection established in the $[a_1, \ldots]$ cases to the $[b_1, \ldots]$ cases.

In the lab case, since the issue involves the effects of a particular chemical compound on the physical condition of the organism in question, we would likely suspect that chimps are more similar to humans in the important respects than cats, salamanders, fireflies, or lima beans would be. Consequently, we would suspect that the connections we saw in chimps are more likely to transfer to humans than connections observed only in cats, salamanders, fireflies, or lima beans. And if the connection was observed not only in chimp cases but also in cat and other cases, it would be even more likely that the connection would hold for humans as well. In addition, any significant disanalogies between the two things or groups that might undercut the plausibility of such a transfer would weaken the argument. Recall the ant extract case.

III. Summary and Conclusion

In analogical arguments we consider two sets of cases we take to be similar in relevant respects and argue that a characteristic known to belong to one will likely belong to the other. We make use of analogical arguments every time we draw a conclusion based on the similarities between things—something we do very often, even if we are not aware of it. Given the role of experience and judgment calls concerning relevant similarities, the assessment of analogical arguments cannot be as definitive as the assessment of deductive arguments. Perhaps that's why some claim that analogical arguments are the weakest form of argument. But the people who say that should fervently hope that they are wrong on this point, since they daily stake their lives on analogical arguments. Remember the dog food case.

10.

Informal Fallacies

The all-too-familiar scene of human carnage and physical devastation following a suicide bombing had been replaced on the TV screen by a picture of a smiling, cheerful-looking young man—the suspected bomber.

Melissa was stunned: "He is—he was—just a kid! Did you see that? He couldn't have been more than 15!"

Andrea seemed unimpressed: "Well, you don't have to apply for an official license and meet an age requirement to murder a bunch of innocent kids at a daycare center. Anyway, what's so surprising about this bombing? Religion has been inspiring hatred and violence ever since religion and hatred and violence were invented."

"But . . . he was just a kid himself." Melissa couldn't get over that fact.

"Well, for some reason, mindless fanaticism seems to be more contagious among young people," Andrea continued. "My theory is that younger people have stronger hormones that overpower their ability to think straight, and as people get older they gradually calm down and outgrow the religious belief that hating and slaughtering anyone with a different view is a wonderful idea."

"You, of course, being an exception to the rule that young people are not able to think straight, I suppose? Anyway, I hope you're not going to try to pretend that all the hatred and wars in the world are religion's fault"—this from René.

"Yeah." said Melissa in support of René, "Anybody who would do something like this to, like, three-year-olds had to be pure evil to begin with, whether or not they were religious."

"No—not evil to begin with. We begin innocent and good, but then something happens—and usually religion is what happens. For instance, take this kid. Probably starting even before he was three, someone began systematically twisting his defenseless little mind with religious teachings until he eventually got to the point where he sincerely thought that doing something like this was right. And who was pulling the strings on his little three-year-old mind? Right—some religious 'authority' feeding him fanatical premises, plausible-sounding but bad logic, and convincing him of the sort of conclusions that resulted in this suicide bombing. Now that was as much child abuse as the bombing was."

"Well, you still can't blame everything on religion. Stalin, Mao, Hitler, Pol Pot, Columbian drug gangs—none of them were motivated by religion. In fact some of them were motivated by a deep hatred of religion." René was digging her heels in.

"Well, either way, rational thinking—reason and logic, especially in the form of science—is the key to moral principles and conduct, and rejecting reason and logic is a guaranteed ticket to mass slaughter. Maybe religion hasn't always been the only guilty party, but it has been right up there—and it has been really good at rejecting reason in favor of blind authority."

"Well, Andrea, as you keep saying, we need to look at the evidence. And so far all you've done is make big sweeping pronouncements—claims that I bet you have accepted uncritically on the authority of influential antireligious bigots. Anyway, even if some religious people are pretty bad at science or reason or logic or whatever, religion certainly doesn't have a monopoly on that problem. My study group has been reading some of the 'New Atheist' books, and a lot of their antireligious arguments are pretty sloppy. Have you read any of them, Andrea? Even if you liked their conclusions, some of their arguments would make you blush."

"Yeah," agreed Melissa. "What René said."

I. Informal Fallacies: The Basic Concept

That religion is to blame for a lot of the world's violence is a charge of long standing. But just how tight is the case against religion case here? No one has actually quantified the amount of violence that religionists vs. atheists have done over the course of history (although some estimates of the number of Stalin's murder victims alone run as high as 60 million people). And no one has done the actual work of separating cases where religion was a cause from those where something else was the actual cause and religion merely served as a handy rhetorical excuse.

So what are the some of the currently popular arguments against religion? How powerful are those arguments? And—more to our present purpose—what can logic tell us about some of those arguments? At the end of this chapter we'll examine an antireligious argument proposed by one of the New Atheists René referred to.

In this chapter we'll review many of the **informal fallacies** we often commit in the course of discussion, disagreement, and debate. "Informal fallacies" is a label for a bag of bad argument types we often use on each other—knowingly or unknowingly—in debate and disagreement. They have proven to be rhetorically effective. They help us score points against our opponents and convince others. That's why they're so common. But they typically employ premises that are either irrelevant or inadequate, or assume too much, or are just plain false. They are faulty types of reasoning and should be exposed as such. Like fouls in a game of basketball, they ought to be called out.

Fallacious deductive arguments usually wear their problems on their sleeve; we can spot their faults by just examining their form. If there is a fallacy present, it will show up as an invalid form. But informal fallacies are different. Here the term *fallacy* is used in a very broad sense, spanning a multitude of sins. Two arguments could employ the same form, yet one could be an instance of an informal fallacy and the other not. Often we have to get inside them, consider their content, if we are to sort them out. We should also note that while informal fallacies do not provide us with good reasons for believing something, their premises can provide us with good reasons for *refraining* from believing something. It would be an informal fallacy on our part to think that because a used car salesman just wants to make a sale, much of what he tells us about a car on his lot must be false. As we'll see, that informal fallacy is known as "poisoning the well." But knowing that a used car salesman just wants to make a sale may legitimately lead us to the conclusion that we should refrain from believing much of what he says is true on his say-so alone.

The wide variety of errors in this area of reasoning has made the systematic classification of informal fallacies notoriously difficult. We will attempt no classification here. We simply present a brief list—by no means comprehensive—of some the most common informal fallacies.

II. Informal Fallacies: A List

Post Hoc Ergo Propter Hoc (**"After this, therefore because of this"**): to claim that because *B* happened after *A*, *A* caused *B*. That may be the case, but we are not justified in believing that *A* caused *B* just because *B* followed *A* in time. This is a species of false cause fallacies in which a cause is incorrectly identified.

Example. I walk into my philosophy class. My professor gives a lecture on Immanuel Kant's transcendental deduction of the categories as found in the A edition of *The Critique of Pure Reason*. I get a headache. After class, I complain that the lecture on Kant gave me a headache.

Assessment. That may be the case. But maybe not. The temporal sequence of the two events (first lecture, then headache) is not in itself an adequate basis for the claim. There are other causal possibilities: maybe the cook in the school cafeteria used MSG in the omelet I had for breakfast, and I'm allergic to MSG. Maybe I failed to have my regular cup of morning coffee before class, and because of my caffeine dependence I got a headache. Maybe maintenance laid a new carpet in the classroom over the weekend, and I'm reacting to the fumes it's giving off.

Correlation Proves Causation: to infer from the regular correlation of two phenomena, *A* and *B*, that *A* must cause *B*, or that *B* must cause *A*. Given the correlation of *A* and *B*, it may be the case that *A* causes *B*; or it may be the case that *B* causes *A*; or it may be the case that *A* and *B* are both caused by a third factor, *C*, a "common cause." The correlation alone cannot tell us which way the causal arrow points; indeed, if the correlation is just a sustained coincidence, there may be no causal arrow that connects the phenomena in question. This is another species of false cause fallacies.

Example. Social research discovers a strong correlation between low levels of education and poverty. "That proves it," one researcher concludes. "Lack of education is one of the chief causes of poverty!"

Assessment. It may be the case that low levels of education is one of the chief causes of poverty. But the strong correlation between low levels of education and poverty alone does not show this. It may be the case that poverty is one of the chief causes of low levels of education. Or it might be the case that both poverty and low levels of education are caused by a third factor. One could imagine a culture that shunned both wealth and higher education as worldly values. In that case both poverty and low levels of education would have been caused largely by a cultural attitude. Hence their correlation.

Hasty Generalization: to make a general claim about some group on the basis of either an inadequate number or an unrepresentative set of examples. Many of the shared characteristics of a small or unrepresentative batch of examples could be a matter of mere coincidence.

Example. I am treated rudely by a bus driver and a waiter in Paris; I email my friends back home, "Parisians are really rude people."

Assessment. Sorry, there are millions of Parisians, and I interacted with only two of them (in perhaps less-than-ideal circumstances). My interaction with two Parisians in these circumstances is not an adequate basis for making a general claim about all, or even most, Parisians.

False Dilemma (aka False Dichotomy): to falsely assume that there are only two alternatives and that if we reject one, we must embrace the other. If there are more than two alternatives, the argument does not guarantee the truth of the conclusion.

Example. "You're not for full-body scanners at the airport? What are you, in favor of terrorists blowing up airplanes?" Here we are presented with just two alternatives: either we are in favor of full-body scanners at the airport, or we're in favor of terrorists blowing up airplanes. Presumably we're not in favor of terrorists blowing up airplanes, so, the reasoning goes, we should be in favor of full-body scanners.

Assessment. The logic of the argument is unassailable: either A or B; not B; therefore, A. If there are only two alternatives and one is eliminated, then the other alternative follows as a matter of strict deduction. The argument form is a disjunctive syllogism, and, as we saw in chapter one, it's valid. The problem here lies in the first premise—there are more alternatives than it puts on offer. More generally, for any false dilemma, however many alternatives, n, it names or assumes, there are at least $n+1$ alternatives. The problem with a false dilemma argument is that it has a false premise. In our case there are more than two alternatives: I could be in favor of security measures that I think are just as effective as but less invasive than full-body scanners. Of course, sometimes there really are only two alternatives, in which case a dilemma argument does not count as an informal fallacy. Not all dilemma arguments are based on false dilemmas.

Begging the Question *(Petitio Principii)***:** to assume precisely what is at issue; it builds the conclusion into one of the premises. Again, on a purely logical level, there is nothing wrong with this kind of argument. If one assumes that P is the case, then of course P follows. But the exercise seems rather pointless. If *P* is what is to be established by the argument because it is controversial, you won't convince anyone by simply starting with the assumption that *P* is true. Pulling a rabbit out of a hat is no big accomplishment if you began by stuffing the rabbit into the hat. But language often helps us pull off the trick: we can redescribe the premise when it appears in the conclusion so that, initially, it doesn't look like we're just asserting what we've already assumed. Yes, I may have stuffed a rabbit in the hat, but what I pulled out was an *Oryctolagus cuniculus*! So the argument is fallacious in the sense that even if it's rhetorically effective, it shouldn't be; it's not entitled to persuade anyone who does not already agree with you on the point under discussion.

Example. "The Bible is God's Word. If you don't believe me, look at 2 Timothy 3:16, where it clearly says that all Scripture is divinely inspired. That means all Scripture is God's Word. Now if the Bible is divinely inspired then it can't be wrong! So it must be God's Word."

Assessment. It may be the case that the Bible is the Word of God. And it may be that the Bible says that it is the Word of God. But if that's the very point under dispute, it will do no good to appeal the authority of the Word of God (redescribed here as "divinely inspired Scripture") in order to establish the authority of the Word of God. To convince a skeptic of this claim, a different case will have to be built.

Usage note: Here "to beg the question" does not mean "to lead us to ask the question," which is how we often find it used in journalistic circles. In philosophy, "to beg the question" means "to assume precisely what is up for debate."

Slippery Slope: to argue that because there is no big difference between any two close points on a continuum, there is no stopping point between two distant points on that continuum. More commonly, it is the idea that one small step in a certain direction will inevitably lead to a process with a big undesirable outcome. This form of reasoning is not always fallacious, but one would have to show that there is a causal or logical connection present that drives the downward slide; the farther apart the beginning and end points of the process are, the stronger the mechanism has to be. Without a case for such a mechanism or logic, the slippery slope argument is at least very weak.

Example. "Start smoking tobacco cigarettes and the next thing you know you'll be smoking marijuana. And after smoking marijuana you'll soon be doing amphetamines, and then it's just a matter of time before you get hooked on the hard drugs like cocaine or heroin. So don't start smoking."

Assessment. There may be very good reasons for not smoking cigarettes. But this alarmist slippery-slope argument is not among them. Many people smoke cigarettes but have not gone from there to an addiction to hard drugs. Here the mechanism that puts us on the slippery slope seems to be lacking. If it had been argued that a person should not start with the occasional use of methamphetamine because it will be just a matter of time before the drug takes over that person's life full-time, then a legitimate point would have been made. Methamphetamine is known to be powerfully addictive; the causal mechanism is present. Again, sometimes we have to get into the content of an argument to see whether it's an informal fallacy.

Definitional Dodge (or Tendentious Stipulation): to redefine a term in an argument in order to circumvent a counterexample. This fallacy is most often committed in connection with defending a general claim. It's an illegitimate way of making a general claim insensitive to empirical evidence.

Example. Initial claim: "Americans are in love with cars and have no interest in the development of public transit." Objection: "Well, I'm an American and I think the development of public transit is a good idea." Response: "Clearly you're not a real American."

Assessment. The initial claim that Americans have no interest in public transit looks like an empirical claim, based perhaps on some sort of social research. But in response to the counterexample, the person who holds this view hangs on to it in spite of empirical evidence to the contrary by just *defining* "American" as "one who has no interest in public transit." This definition is tendentious. It's an instance of special pleading. Look up "American" in the dictionary, you will not find "one who has no interest in public transit" as one of the definitions.

Against the Person (*Ad Hominem*): to attack the person rather than the argument. This kind of argument suffers from the problem of irrelevance. Negative facts about a person do not count as good reasons for believing that the claims made by that person are in fact false (unless the negative fact is that the person is a pathological liar!).

Example. "Harry claims that concerns about social justice are motivated by envy, that poor people want what rich people have and therefore want the government to take from the rich to give to the poor in the name of fairness. Well, he should know; twelve years ago he was down on his luck and found guilty of robbing a bank!"

Assessment. Harry's criminal record is not relevant to the evaluation of his political views or the quality of his arguments. Law-abiding citizens can have false political views and bad arguments for them; hardened criminals can have true political views and good arguments for them. One must turn to the reasons Harry has for his claim, not to his criminal record.

You Too! *(Tu Quoque)*: to deflect an argument by claiming that the other person does the same kind of thing for which one is being criticized. This is a form of *ad hominem* argument but is typically used in defense of one's own position or behavior.

Example. You eat at a restaurant with a friend. After paying your bill, you realize that the server gave you too much in change— $12.00 instead of $2.00. You decide not to return the extra amount. On the way out, your friend says you really ought to give the money back. You respond: "Who are you to object? You don't always pay what you owe either. Last year, I paid you $200 for some work around the house and you said you weren't going to report it as income on your tax return."

Assessment. That your friend committed a similar wrong does not make what you did right or even permissible. At best, it would show that what you did is not unusual; but it is irrelevant to the moral evaluation of your action.

Poisoning the Well: to suggest that we should take a statement to be false because of the suspect motives or bad faith of the person who proposes it. This is also a type of *ad hominem* argument. A person's suspect motives for making a claim are not good reasons for believing that the claim is false. But again, they might be good reasons for refraining from believing that the claim is true on that person's say-so alone. If a person or organization stands to benefit greatly from having others believe some particular proposition, it doesn't follow that the proposition in question is false. But knowing that a person or organization stands to benefit greatly from having others believe some particular proposition might be a good reason to reserve judgment.

Example. "BP claims that the waters of the Gulf of Mexico are now as clean as can be, and that they've completely repaired all the damage done by that oil spill. Sure! That just can't be true. BP has everything to gain from the good publicity created by that claim."

Assessment. BP may be entirely correct in its claim about the waters of the Gulf of Mexico, even it if stands to benefit greatly if people believe that claim. At most, we should withhold belief on that point—given the material interests of the party that made it—and look for independent evidence.

Straw Man (aka Straw Person): to misrepresent an opponent's position—knowingly or unknowingly—so that it is easier to refute. A straw man is easier to beat in a boxing match; an extreme position is easier to refute in debate. The problem is this: in refuting the misrepresented position one has not refuted the actual position.

Example. Let's say a person believes that the state should not outlaw corporal punishment as a form of discipline exercised by parents over their children. "What?" says the person who disagrees, "you want parents to beat their kids senseless every time a rule is broken? You've got to be nuts!"

Assessment. Clearly this is an attempt to misrepresent the person's position, which is only that not all forms of corporal punishment ought to be criminalized. Such a person might make a distinction between corporal punishment and child abuse and hold that the latter should be and remain against the law. Such a person might think that all forms of corporeal punishment are in fact immoral or counterproductive, and should not be practiced, but that it would be a bad idea to make them all illegal. This is a far cry from advocating child abuse.

Loaded Words: to try to make a person's position look bad by hanging negative words on it (e.g., "bizarre," "infantile," "fascist," "socialist," "cretinous," "perverted," "pea-brained," "muttonheaded," "risible").

Example. "You say the Chicago Cubs are going to win the pennant this year? Why, that's the most ridiculous, bizarre, and outlandish view I've heard for a long time! What a joke!"

Assessment. Ridiculing the belief just shows us that you don't like it. If you come out against the belief, we already know that. Rather than ridiculing the belief, one should assess the evidence. For instance, at a certain point in the baseball season, it may be mathematically impossible for the Cubs to win the pennant; or at the beginning of the season all the numbers—the ERAs of the Cubs' pitchers, the RBIs of their batters—may be so dismal as to make the make the belief that the Cubs will win the pennant unjustified in the extreme. Note: Loaded words can also be used to make a position look good (e.g., "noble," "high-minded," "truly

American," "deeply Christian," "even-handed," "unbiased," "brilliant," "luminous," "stunning"). Rather than trying to make a position look good by dressing it up in glowing terms, one should examine the reasons for it.

Fallacy of Composition: to reason from properties of the parts to a property of the whole made up of those parts; it transfers the properties of the parts to the whole made up of those parts. But the whole need not have properties possessed by each of the parts. We cannot automatically assume that's the case.

Example. "You like vanilla ice cream, right? You like roasted eggplant, right? You like caramel, right? And you like sardines, right? Well, I've got the perfect dessert for you: a sardine, roasted-eggplant, and caramel sundae!"

Assessment. It may be true that someone likes each of these parts individually; but it just doesn't follow that they like them all together. The whole is a new entity that they may or may not like. Here too, however, whether composition is a fallacy or not depends on the content of the claims. One can legitimately infer that since of all the exterior body parts of a car are painted green, the exterior of the car as a whole is painted green.

The Fallacy of Division: to reason from the properties of the whole to the properties of the parts; it transfers a property of the whole to all of its parts. This is the reverse of the fallacy of composition. The parts need not have the properties of the whole.

Example. "Please be sure to give Mr. Welks a good welcome. He comes from one of the most prestigious and tech-savvy companies in Europe. So roll out the red carpet. He'll be one of the most prestigious and tech-savvy visitors we've had in a long time."

Assessment. Mr. Welks may belong to one of the most prestigious and tech-savvy companies in Europe—that's the whole of which he is a part—but that doesn't make him prestigious and tech-savvy. He could be an assistant to the associate of the company's event coordinator and know very little about technology. Like composition, however, whether division is a fallacy depends on the content of the claims: if the whole shirt is made in Indonesia, then the sleeves of the shirt were made in Indonesia.

Appeal to the Gallery: to support a position by excessive appeal to what the majority thinks or feels about the matter. What the majority of people think or feel is often sensible, but appealing to it in the face of a specific argument or evidence is to avoid the issue.

Example. "Well, I know a retired lieutenant colonel in the Air Force recently said there were two UFO crashes in Roswell, New Mexico, back in 1947. And yeah, they've got some metal parts with funny writing on them in a bag. But the good people of America don't believe in little green men hopping out of saucers, and neither should you."

Assessment. To appeal to what the good people of American believe in the face of specific evidence is to draw attention away from precisely what stands in need of evaluation. The majority can be wrong after all. On the other hand, the evidence put forward may be very shaky. But we won't know that until it is addressed and assessed.

The Red Herring: to distract attention from the issue under discussion by introducing a new element that is, strictly speaking, unrelated. The argument, then, is beside the point. Some think the name for this fallacy derives from the practice of using smoked herring to distract hunting dogs from the trail of the prey.

Example. "You say that our teachers need to be assessed on a regular basis if we are to improve the schools. But what about the students? Are we doing a good job in assessing the students on a regular basis?"

Assessment. It appears this person is against new assessments for teachers, but argues against them by trying to shift the discussion to the assessment of students. That's a separate topic.

Appeal to Irrelevant Authority: to resort to the opinions of an authority figure on a topic outside his or her area of expertise. Accepting beliefs on the basis of authority is generally a good idea, and we do it all the time. We listen to our mechanic to find out what's wrong with our car; we listen to our teacher to find out about the history of the First World War; we learn from our language instructor about how to form the subjunctive in German. This is not to say that authorities always get things right or that they never abuse their position. Human expertise and authority is limited. Authorities may know some things, but not all things. We should not appeal to authority in areas where that authority has no expertise. We find the inappropriate appeal to authority often in advertising, where people accomplished in one field will give us consumer advice in a totally unrelated field. Similarly, well-known scientists might be cited for their religious opinions, or musicians consulted for their views on foreign policy. In these cases, it is likely that whatever authority and expertise they may have acquired is irrelevant to the issue at hand. And in areas where credible authorities disagree, we should exercise caution.

Example. Sally Field, a two-time Oscar-winning actress known for her roles in *Lincoln, Places in the Heart,* and *Norma Rae,* is also known for her work in television ads recommending Boniva, a prescription bisphosphonate drug used in the treatment of osteoporosis.

Assessment. Of course people can give testimonials for something they feel has worked for them. Television ads for Chantrix, a smoking cessation drug, feature ordinary folks. What additional value does Sally Field bring to the Boniva ads? It would seem that her skills, accomplishments, and renown as an actress bring no special expertise to the field of medicine. Should we be especially motivated to request that drug from our doctor on her say-so? Medical studies have indicated that bisphosphonates can reduce the risk of hip and spine fractures, but other studies have suggested that such drugs can also increase the likelihood of thighbone fractures. If we wanted advice on this drug, given its possible benefits and potential side effects, it would pay to place more credence in an informed interpreter of clinical studies, well-studied in the field of pharmacology.

Argument from Ignorance: to claim that a good reason for believing something is true is that is has not been proven false; or that a good reason for believing something is false is that it has not been proven true. If something has been rightly shown to be false, then it is false. But if it has not been shown to be false, it doesn't follow that it is true. In the absence of any other evidence, we should just maintain that we don't know if it's true or false. And the same holds vice versa: if something has not been shown to be true, it doesn't follow that it's false.

Example. "Sure, garlic helps keep your bad cholesterol numbers down. There is not a single clinical study conducted in the United States or in Europe that contradicts this fact."

Assessment. Again, it doesn't follow from the fact that it has not been shown to be false that garlic reduces bad cholesterol numbers that garlic does reduce bad cholesterol numbers. What we need is positive evidence that it reduces those numbers.

Equivocation: to use a key term first with one meaning and then with another meaning in the course of an argument. Many words have more than one meaning. The word *blue*, for instance, can be used to refer to a color or a mood. Multiple meanings attaching to the same word can give rise to ambiguity and equivocation. In logic it is important to avoid both. Ambiguity arises in statements using a word that has more than one meaning, and the meaning of the word is not nailed down by the statement in which it appears. Ambiguity helps poets get extra mileage from the words they use, and it makes for great jokes involving puns, but in logic and the assessment of arguments it can be the cause of much mischief. It can make it difficult to tell whether a statement is true, or whether an argument is legitimate. Take, for instance, the claim "Harrison Ford loses appeal." This statement could mean that Harrison Ford just lost an appeal in a recent court case, or it could mean that he's lost his sex appeal as an actor. Here's another example (a real headline): "Juvenile Court to Try Shooting Defendant." Sometimes sentences themselves are ambiguous because of their grammatical construction. For example: "Feike Feikema never argues with his father when he's drunk." Does this mean that Feike Feikema never argues with his father when he—Feike Feikema—is drunk, or that Feike Feikema never argues with his father when he—his father—is drunk? It's hard to tell. Here's another one (a real headline): "Enraged Cow Injures Farmer with Ax." Technically, a grammatical structure that makes the meaning of a sentence ambiguous is known as an *amphiboly*.

Equivocation happens when a key term shifts meaning in the course of an argument. When this happens, the premises don't add up to support the conclusion; they're not tracking the same thing.

Example. Consider the following argument:

1. Only man is a rational animal.
2. A woman is not a man.
3. Therefore, a woman is not a rational animal.

Assessment. Here the word *man* shifts from being a generic term for all humans in the first statement to a gender-specific term in the second statement. Technically, an argument like this must restrict itself to the use of three terms (here: "man," "woman," and "rational"). But equivocation on the word *man* creates four terms ("man [humankind]," "man [males]," "woman," and "rational"). The equivocation renders the argument defective. The first premise of the argument uses "man" in the generic sense, and the second uses "man" in the gender-specific sense, so the premises do not add up to support the conclusion. They're not about the same thing when they use the key term "man."

III. Assessment of an Example

Over lunch you went to the CNN website to catch up on the news. Another report of an attack on innocent civilians motivated by religious conflict. Another suicide bombing. You recall reading a story just last week of a church group attending a military funeral, informing those in mourning that God hated them. You wonder: Has religion really made the world a better place? Maybe we'd be better off without it. Oddly, snippets from a John Lennon song start playing in your head: "Imagine there's no heaven ... and no religion too ... nothing to live or die for. ... Imagine all the people living life in peace . . . and the world will be as one." Returning to your room, you notice a book on your roommate's shelf: *God Is Not Great: How Religion Poisons Everything*, by the journalist and literary critic Christopher Hitchens. It seems timely. You open to the chapter entitled "Does Religion Make People Behave Better?" You read with interest. There Hitchens cites several examples of evil committed by religious individuals or institutions: (1) The Anglo-Catholic author Evelyn Waugh supported fascist movements; (2) in Uganda, Joseph Kony led the Lord's Resistance Army, committing all sorts of atrocities in the name of religion; (3) the Catholic Church was complicit in the persecution of the Tutsis in Rwanda. His conclusion: "This makes it impossible to argue that religion causes people to behave in a more kindly or civilized manner" (p. 192).

Maybe he's got a point, you think. But then, he only cites three examples where people have done bad things in the name of religion, or where religion evidently failed to keep people from doing bad things, in order to get to that claim about religion in general. But, you think, religious people have done millions of things; and millions of things have been done in the name of religion. Were they all evil? You've studied some history. Right off the top of your head you can think of some examples of good things people have done in the name of religion, or, at least, good things religious people have done: William Wilberforce, the English Victorian Christian, worked for the abolition of the slave trade in the English Empire; Dietrich Bonhoeffer, the German Lutheran theologian, opposed fascism in his own country during the Second World War; Dr. Martin Luther King Jr., the American Baptist preacher, led the civil rights movement in the 1960s. It seems like these actions would be weighty counterexamples against the claim the religion fails to make people behave in a more kindly or civilized manner. Maybe Hitchens would have to modify his claim.

You read more. He doesn't. Instead, he makes the striking claim that insofar as these people did something good, they were not religious. Dietrich Bonhoeffer, in opposing Hitler, subscribed to a "nebulous humanism" (p. 7). And Martin Luther King Jr.? "In no real sense was he a Christian," Hitchens claims (p. 176). Rev. King took his stand for civil rights as a "profound humanist" (p. 180). Then you think to yourself: It looked like Hitchens's claim that religion fails to make people morally better is an empirical claim, a claim based on the observation and collection of facts about how religious people actually behave. Are there no facts a person could cite concerning the behavior of religious people or institutions that would challenge his general claim? Something fishy is going on here. But what?

Clearly the claim that religion fails to improve people, based on three examples, is a hasty generalization. The examples he gives are vivid—lending his point some rhetorical punch—but woefully in adequate in number. Again: religious people have done millions of things, and people have done millions of things in the name of religion. Three things—even 30 things—do not constitute a sufficient sample. (Even 30,000 examples would be inadequate if they were cherry-picked for their negative qualities. They would be unrepresentative.)

Not content to give up this fallacy, Hitchens defends it with another, the definitional dodge. The claim that religion fails to make people better and generally makes people worse appears to be an empirical claim, a claim based on observation. But when confronted with evidence to the contrary, it becomes clear that it is not an empirical claim at all. Hitchens has just decided to *define* religion from the outset as that which makes people worse. Even the subtitle of his book, *How Religion Poisons Everything*, suggests that religion not only fails to make things better, it makes things worse; it's not just an ineffective remedy, it's a deadly poison. If a belief makes someone better, then by his definition it's not religion but rather humanism (the view he wants to promote). He gives himself this point through the simple expedient of defining his terms to suit his purpose.

This move brings to mind a story that a philosopher by the name of O. K. Bouwsma once told when responding to a similar ploy in a philosophical debate: Once upon a time, a vacuum salesman demonstrated a vacuum cleaner to the woman of the house (this story was told in the 1950s). "Ma'am, this vacuum is so powerful that it will pick up all the dirt off your carpet." He ran the vacuum over the carpet. The woman inspected the carpet, noticed some dirt the vacuum failed to clean, and pointed it out. "You said the vacuum cleaner would pick up all the dirt off the carpet. But look, here's some dirt." "Oh no, ma'am," the salesman protested, "if this vacuum doesn't pick it up, it's not dirt!"

IV. Summary and Conclusion

Informal fallacies are a rag-tag bunch of bad arguments we often use on each other in discussion and debate. The ones described in this chapter are used so often they even have their own names. However common they may be, it is hard to characterize what's wrong with them in a single phrase. Some of them are valid deductive arguments, but with false premises (the False Dilemma); some of them are valid deductive arguments where the premises may even be true (Begging the Question); some of them are inductive arguments, but based on a small or unrepresentative sample (the Hasty Generalization); some of them make use of reasons that are entirely irrelevant to the issue at hand (Ad Hominem, the Red Herring, Loaded Words, Poisoning the Well); some of them are fallacies sometimes, but not other times, depending on their content (the Slippery Slope). Some of them are most commonly used in the defense of a position (the Definitional Dodge), while others are used in the attack of another position (the Straw Man). In addition, some of them are often innocent mistakes in reasoning. One can move from the regular correlation of two phenomena to unfounded causal claims without malicious intent (False Cause). Yet others are often signs that the one who employs them has decided to win an argument by any means—fair or foul. The Ad Hominem, the Straw Man, Poisoning the Well and Loaded Words, we suspect, often fall into this category. We will have more to say about the use and abuse of arguments, and the attitudes that lie behind them, in the concluding chapter on the ethics of argument.

11.

Explanation

It's 3:00 in the morning. Something woke you. You lie quietly, listening intently, then hear a very soft noise, right across the room. You slowly open your eyes and very carefully turn your head just slightly enough to see—very dimly—the other side of the dark room. As your night vision kicks in, you see your roommate, fully dressed, quietly and methodically going through your purse. You involuntarily scream, thereby nearly giving your roommate and yourself heart attacks.

Your roommate's behavior has raised some questions in your mind. You want an *explanation*. And it had better be good. Well, the explanation *is* good. Your roommate had been downstairs studying late for a big exam and developed a ferocious headache. She had come into the room quietly, hoping not to disturb you, to get her ibuprofen out of the purse that (you had momentarily forgotten) you had given her the day before because she had admired it so much. Learning that, you can now relax. All the previously puzzling pieces now fit into a coherent and very sensible overall picture. You now understand your roommate's action.

I. Explanation: The Basic Concept

As the above case suggests, explanations are what provide us with materials for understanding. Your roommate's explanation involved—explicitly or implicitly—her experiencing a headache; her desire to be rid of it; her belief that taking the ibuprofen would lead by ordinary neurophysiological processes to the desired result; a belief that there were ibuprofen tablets in her lovely new purse; a belief that you were a light sleeper; a desire not to disturb your sleep; and so on. In light of this information she made a perfectly sensible decision that gave rise to her behavior. Given your new background information (the *explanans* in her explanation), we would expect—or at the least we would not be surprised—that she behaved the way she did (the *explanandum* of her explanation, the phenomenon you wanted to be explained). We already have a familiarity with common patterns of human behavior (e.g., that most people take ibuprofen, aspirin, or acetaminophen to relieve headaches); we already have a grasp of some basic criteria of rational human decisions. Once we see your roommate's beliefs, desires, and intentions against that background context, the mystery of her behavior is resolved. We now see it fitting quite naturally into a larger, cohesive, familiar sort of picture. To see it in this way, to see it clicking into place within a larger, familiar pattern, is to *understand* it—it makes perfect sense. That's exactly what you were looking for in that early morning episode, and that's what the explanation was intended to produce.

Here's another example: we begin to understand why inflated balloons expand if heated when we are given the information that air consists of molecules (little bits of matter sort of like miniature billiard balls, we were told), and that heating the balloon makes the air molecules inside it bounce around more energetically, hitting the interior walls of the balloon faster, pushing on the walls harder. Given our background familiarity with the everyday pattern of the effects of one thing hitting and pushing harder against something else, we see that the expansion of the balloon is a natural consequence of heating the balloon. Now it makes sense. We understand why balloons expand when heated. Given the new information (the *explanans*) we now recognize the previously puzzling expansion (the *explanandum*) as exemplifying a familiar natural pattern we already grasp.

As the above two examples suggest, explanations often involve very different topics, very different circumstances, very different sorts of *explanans*, very different background patterns, very different pictures, and very different requirements for what will count as a good explanation. The explanation in the first example above involves beliefs, desires, intentions, and familiar patterns of reasonable *human* behavior. The second example includes nothing like that. That explanation appeals to molecules, motions, impacts, heat, and to familiar patterns of purely *physical* processes in nature.

But in most cases explanations nonetheless have the same basic structure: they make sense out of something by providing us with information that, in the context of our background knowledge, allows us to see the thing we want to understand as part of a larger cohesive picture, a picture whose overall patterns are already familiar to us. This general conception of explanation is often referred to as the "covering law" model of explanation: the fact to be explained is seen as falling under a natural law, some other type of natural regularity, or under some established pattern of human behavior.

The above cases also show that explanation typically has a kind of "directional flow." For example, once you add all the new information about your roommate's circumstances to your own background knowledge of patterns of reasonable human behavior, your mind naturally tracks further along such patterns and may even suggest the action she in fact took. Indeed, that action might well have been the action your own thinking would have suggested to you in similar circumstances. Movement along that pattern, starting with *explanans* and going on to *explanandum*, is part of what it means for the explanation to make sense to us. Similarly, once the information about air molecules and their behavior is added to your own background knowledge of patterns of nature involving physical objects and the effects of their impact, your mind naturally tracks further along such natural patterns and can often anticipate the very phenomenon you wish to understand.

However, the connections between *explanans* and *explananda* and the specific tracks between them may be quite different in different sorts of explanations. Part of the reason for this is that, as some philosophers say, an explanation is an answer to a "why?" question, and "why?" questions with respect to human action typically ask for and require different sorts of answers than "why?" questions with respect to natural physical events. In the examples above, for instance, we are looking for human reasons in the first case and for causal laws in the second. Nevertheless, the overall explanatory structure is basically the same in both cases.

At this point we might wonder why explanations are coming up in a book on logic. Logic, after all, deals primarily with arguments. We use arguments to convince others *that* something is the case, not *why* it is the case. One reason for the inclusion of this topic is that explanations sometimes resemble arguments so closely that for decades many philosophers thought explanations just were a special type of argument. One of the important parallels involves the directional flow mentioned earlier. In scientific explanations, for instance, there is usually a *causal* track that the mind pursues from *explanans* to *explanandum*; in arguments there is an *inferential* track that the mind pursues from premises to conclusion.

There are, however, important differences between arguments and explanations, and it is no longer widely believed that explanations are just a species of argument. One significant difference is that the connections ultimately underlying the tracks that the mind follows out are quite different in the two cases. Explanations typically involve causation (sometimes called "natural necessity"), while arguments (in their deductive form) involve logical necessity.

Another important difference is the one we just alluded to: whereas arguments are generally intended to convince us *that* something is true, explanations are generally intended to help us see *why* something is true. For instance, on the basis of various arguments you may come to believe that it is true that global warming is indeed occurring. But after becoming convinced of that, you might next wonder *why* it is occurring, *why* it is true, what accounts for that warming, what is causally driving that warming. Various people for various reasons have advanced competing explanations: human activity, solar cycles, geological cycles, even alien activity.

Despite these differences in character and aim, there are significant connections between explanations and arguments. One important connection has to do with the question of why, when confronted with multiple possible explanations, we should accept one explanation over the others. What justifies us in taking one explanation to be better than its competitors? How can we tell which one is better? One influential answer to this question is called **inference to the best explanation** (IBE). Inferences are based on arguments. Arguments, then, might convince us that one explanation, one answer to a "why" question, is the best of all the explanations on offer.

What kinds of arguments support IBE? There are good and bad, better and worse explanations. An explanation can be defective in having some of its alleged facts wrong, in relying upon some problematic background assumptions, in taking something to be a pattern in human behavior or in physical nature when it actually is not, in depending upon some improper or overly sketchy track between the *explanans* and the *explanandum*, or in a variety of other ways. In the current climate debate, some contend that explanations citing anthropogenic (human-driven) causes of global warming are defective in various ways; others contend that explanations citing natural cycles as causes are the defective ones. Oddly, most claim to find something wrong with the alien explanation. Yet some deny that there is even anything to be explained, that there simply is no global warming, that there is no *explanadum* in this case.

Granted that there is something to explain, how do we settle these disputes over which explanation is the best explanation? The problem is especially tricky in cases where proposed explanations involve theoretical matters, things we cannot directly observe—quarks, the deep cosmic past, processes in the center of the sun, air molecules, other people's intentions, murders when there is no body, and the like. In such cases, just looking to find out which explanation is the right one is not an option. Then what do we do?

In general, we look for explanations that have characteristics we believe make them more likely to be correct explanations, more likely to help us truly understand reality. We generally take such explanations to be among those that are simpler, that are clearer, that give us more precise detail, that lead us to more accurate expectations concerning new situations, that apply in a wider range of situations than competing theories, and that involve patterns and background assumptions in which we already have some confidence because they have proven to be reliable in the past. According to IBE, in some cases we are rationally warranted in inferring that the best of our available competing explanations, judged by these criteria, is in fact the correct explanation.

There are obvious pitfalls here. We could be wrong about what makes one explanation good or better than other explanations. And there are disagreements on this point. Our background assumptions might be skewed. In many cases there are disputes about which assumptions are the right ones. An even more troubling worry is that the right explanation might not be among those on offer, and that our best explanation might still be far wrong. Indeed, we are fallible, limited human beings with all sorts of cognitive weaknesses. And we—including scientists, philosophers, and theologians—have been wrong in the past. So even if we can figure out and agree on which explanation is best, how can we be justified taking our current *best* explanation to be the *right* explanation? Or even probably right?

These are genuine problems, and they are among the reasons why the results of scientific explanation and inference can never be taken for complete certainty, as if they gave us absolute guarantees of truth. But we have little choice other than to do the best we can with our wonderful capabilities as well as our sobering limitations. And that is indeed the rational thing to do. For the religiously minded there is at least some encouragement to be found in the belief that we were created to inhabit this world knowingly, created to be responsible creatures capable of knowledge within our own environment.

II. Assessing Explanations

As noted earlier, explanations are typically answers to "why" questions. But such questions are ambiguous. Recall the first example, your roommate with the headache. Making sense of her behavior required references to her beliefs, desires, intentions, decisions, and the like. In the second example, the expanding balloon, making sense of the expansion involved reference to physical microstructures, molecular dynamics, cause and effect, and the like. There are other categories of explanation, but these two—taking "why" as purpose, and taking "why" as cause—are the most prominent.

In both cases we seek to make sense of initially mysterious phenomena. In both cases we do that by embedding the phenomena within a narrative. Making sense of the two cases required an *agent* narrative and a *causal* narrative, respectively. In the one we try to make sense of the phenomena by constructing a narrative of desires, purposes, beliefs, reasons, decisions, and such, that fits into previously recognized patterns of reasoning and intentionally driven behaviors of persons. In the other case we try to make sense of the phenomena by constructing a narrative of mechanisms, materials, physical structures, forces, and such, that can be embedded in previously recognized patterns of causally driven physical behaviors of objects. Explanations that meet those conditions make sense to us, although given the profound differences between the two types, it is not surprising that they require different approaches to the criteria for what constitutes a good explanation.

There is no complete list of evaluative criteria for explanations, but among the more important ones are the following:

C1. *Plausibility*: the explanation must make sense (i.e., it must be woven into a plausible narrative that makes connections with identifiable aspects of reality).

C2. *Broad consistency*: the proposed explanation must be generally consistent with other things we know—both other facts and more general principles.

C3. *Relevance*: there must be adequate connections (not necessarily deductive) between *explanans* and *explanandum*;

given the *explanans*, we should expect the *explanandum*, or at least the initial puzzlement of the *explanandum* should be removed.

C4. *Simplicity*: the explanation should not be more complex than it needs to be.

C5. *Empirical accuracy*: if the explanatory theory makes or allows further specific predictions (and not all good theories do), those predictions must be correct for the most part.

Frequently there are a number of competing explanations for the puzzles that confront us. The explanation that fares best on the above criteria is typically the one we would consider to be the best.

III. An Assessment Example

Most of us would take the earlier explanations of your roommate's behavior and of the expansion of the balloon to be good explanations. But let's look at another example with the above evaluative criteria before us. Consider global warming. Nearly everyone now admits that global warming is occurring. But there are huge debates (also warming) over the right explanation of this phenomenon. There are several competing proposals, including the following:

A. Normal cyclical climactic fluctuations (we're just entering a warming phase)

B. Increased solar energy output (solar energy is being converted into earth heat)

C. Human-produced (anthropogenic) greenhouse gasses (CO_2 and a number of others)

D. The earth entering a region of space containing unusual concentrations of cosmic dust, that dust being gravitationally swept up by the earth and acting as a heat trap

E. Methane produced by cows and other ruminants

F. The ever-popular but elusive aliens, heating the planet to their preferred temperature prior to takeover

The alien proposal (F) runs into serious difficulty with plausibility criterion (C1). The narrative in question seems neither very plausible nor at all properly connected to any identifiable aspect of reality. A plausible alien narrative here would need both agent and causal elements. Unfortunately, aside from the claims of self-appointed alien "experts" on late-night radio talk shows, there seem to be few reliable insights into alien psychology (even if we grant the existence of aliens). The simplicity criterion (C4) also probably counts against proposal F—none of the competing explanations require anything so complex as a technologically advanced, space-conquering, secretive civilization of aliens with strange technologies, physiologies, and psychologies. The alternative theories require only the continuation or augmentation of already known processes (e.g., nature continuing in its thermal cycles, humans continuing to pollute the atmosphere, cows continuing their digestive processes, or cosmic dust continuing to sift through the atmosphere).

Note that proposal F is actually an agent explanation of global warming. It refers to the intentions of aliens, but it does not tell us the specific causal mechanism by which those intentions to bring about the warming of the earth are being achieved. Perhaps they have heat-ray projectors or something equally effective. Agent explanations and causal explanations are frequently separated because it seems that although such things as purposes and reasons prompt behavior, they are not in any mechanical sense *causes*. Still, the two can be interconnected. That possibility is often emphasized in discussions of the relation between science and religion. For instance, some Christians argue that with respect to the diversity of species we can give *both* an agent explanation (God's intentions in the creation) *and* a causal explanation (natural selection as the causal mechanism by which God's intentions are realized).

Most of the remaining global warming proposals above can be—and have been—woven into sensible narratives (C1). Most also pass the relevance criterion (C3) and the simplicity criterion (C4) as well. But the remaining criteria are more problematic for most of them. Given the known geological range of fluctuations, given the known current level of solar energy output, given the best current cosmic-dust evidence, and given the best reasonable estimates of ruminant flatulence, proposed explanations involving climate cycles (A), solar energy (B), cosmic dust (D), and methane gas emitted by animals (E) do not fare well with the consistency criterion (C2), and several do not do well in terms of the empirical accuracy criterion (C5) either. So far as the overwhelming bulk of climate scientists can tell, at this point the proposal that cites human activity (C) does better on all five criteria than any of the other proposed explanations. And in terms of the consistency and empirical accuracy criteria

(C2 and C5), it continues to get increasingly stronger. Consequently, the proposal that cites greenhouse gases produced by human beings represents the current consensus of climatologists and other relevant scientific experts (atmospheric physicists and the like).

Of course, that consensus does not *prove* that proposal C is correct. There are several important reasons for this, as noted earlier. Here are just four of them. First, at any given time the range of explanatory theories we have to choose from is limited. The correct explanation may be one that humans haven't thought of—and perhaps never will think of, perhaps cannot even grasp. It's possible that one of you may someday win a Nobel Prize for coming up with a brilliant, vastly better explanatory narrative (C1) that no one before you has come close to thinking of and that outshines all other proposals on the remaining criteria as well.

Second, at any given time human knowledge is incomplete. Lots of proposals may be consistent with everything we currently know (C2) but not consistent with other, still unknown aspects of reality. In fact, new evidence may turn up next year that creates nearly insurmountable difficulties under the consistency criteria (C2) and the empirical accuracy criteria (C5). Some new conceptual breakthrough may shed new light on the problem and suddenly make one of the other proposed explanations appear to be the best.

Third, applications of the criteria are not straightforward. Most of the criteria come in degrees. A narrative may make more sense than some and less than others; connections may be more or less adequate; and there are many degrees of complexity. Beyond that, the various criteria do not always point to the same explanation. For instance, one proposed explanation may offer slightly more adequate connections (C3) but involve significantly more complexity (C4) than another proposal. And there may be no way to settle which of two conflicting criteria is more crucial.

Fourth, whether a phenomenon is initially puzzling, whether a proposed explanatory narrative is plausible, whether the narrative alleviates that puzzlement, what constitutes complexity—the answers to questions such as these are rooted in factors of human cognition, even human psychology and human physiology. There is of course significant dispute over why we should think that human cognition, psychology, and physiology are keyed to reality in such a way that what makes sense to us, what seems adequate to us, what removes puzzlement for us should be a clue to explanatory truth. That is a difficult question to answer, and any answer will refer us yet again to larger narratives. Some have thought that unguided evolutionary processes have fitted the human mind to the world. Religious traditions have long argued that humans were created as beings capable of knowledge and thus reflect the image of a rational creator. There are other narratives as well. Such narratives may provide us with some hope that our faculties can point us toward truth if carefully, correctly, and humbly used. Which narrative we should adopt may again be in part a matter of an inference to the best explanation.

IV. Explaining Away

When do good explanations not only explain things but explain things away? This could be an important question if you have some investment in the existence or nonexistence of the things up for explanatory dismissal. Consider some simple examples. A few years ago huge, complex geometric diagrams began mysteriously appearing overnight in wheat fields in England. The unexplained appearances of these "crop circles" created a worldwide sensation and all sorts of explanations were proposed. UFO enthusiasts attributed the crop circles to the work of aliens, although why aliens might want to travel trillions of miles to draw circles in selected English fields after dark was not wholly clear. But fairly soon an alternative proposed explanation emerged: a couple middle-aged English pranksters admitted responsibility for the circles. The pranksters in question demonstrated how they had made the circles, and provided other detailed evidence as well. Except to some UFO holdouts, the new explanation was considered a more plausible, better-supported explanation, and it rapidly supplanted the alien explanation. In this case, explanation in terms of alleged activity of aliens was replaced by explanation in terms of activity of humans. The alien activity was explained away.

Explaining away is a fairly familiar occurrence. For instance, at one point in history the apparent motion of the planets was explained in terms of angels or similar celestial beings pushing them along their path. That motion was subsequently explained in terms of purely physical process with no reference to angelic activity. The alleged angelic activity was explained away. Or suppose that in the middle of the night you hear some strange sounds downstairs. "Burglars!" you immediately think, explaining the noise in terms of the nefarious activity of intruders. But when you go down to investigate, you find that the cat had decided to have her kittens on the couch, and in the process she kicked your philosophy books to the floor. Explanation of the noises in terms of alleged activity of burglars has now been supplanted by a different, better, and better-supported explanation: the cat's activity. The alleged burglar has been explained away.

Several things are involved in explaining something away. Here are some of the more important factors exhibited in the above examples:

F1. The initial explanation (E_1) is replaced by a better explanation (E_2).

F2. The replacement explanation (E_2) is supported as well or better by available evidence than the initial explanation (E_1) is.

F3. The replacement explanation (E_2) does not involve the key components of the initial explanation (E_1), which have no explanatory role in the new explanation (E_2).

In the cat case above, the cat explanation is better than the burglar explanation in terms of the evaluative criteria listed above (C1–C5). It is in general more plausible, fits better with our past experiences, is simpler, and so forth, just as F1 specifies. It is better supported by the evidence: the cat is visibly there, visibly producing kittens; the books are visibly on the floor; there are no broken locks or windows, nothing is missing, no burglars are to be seen, and so on, just as F2 indicates. The crucial component of the burglar explanation—a burglar—plays no role in the new explanation, in accord with F3. So we relax, coo over the cuteness of the new kittens, and no longer believe in the existence—much less the activity—of the initially proposed burglars. The alleged burglars and the alleged larcenous activity have been explained away. But the things you were trying to explain (the *explanandum*, those noises) have not been explained away. They were real. You heard them. Nothing in the new explanation casts any doubt on them. Indeed, they are now *explained*, not explained *away*. But the initial explanation—the one involving the activity of burglars—is no longer accepted.

The same is true of the other cases above, and you can pretty easily see that all three criteria are met in those cases as well. In the crop circle case, although the things being explained—crop circles—are still very real, the core of the initial explanation—alien activity—no longer plays any role in the best explanation. It has been explained away. And the same holds for the case of the angels. The motion of the planets is still acknowledged, but the crux of the initial explanation—angels pushing the planets—plays no role in the new explanation. That activity too has been explained away.

Not all such proposed cases, however, are so straightforward. There are lots of disputed cases, but in such cases the disputes are typically over whether the above criteria are met, whether the proposed alternative explanation really is better, whether it really is better supported, or whether it really is independent of the key aspects of the initial explanation.

V. Undercutting Apparent Rationality

In some cases we can take explaining away one step further. In the alleged burglar case, the only reason for initially believing that there was a burglar downstairs was that a burglar would explain the unusual noises you were hearing. The burglar idea was your theory to account for what you had heard. The burglar was your explanatory hypothesis for the noises, and it may have been a good initial explanation. But once the cat explanation and its strong supporting evidence was discovered, and the burglar explanation was superseded by a much better explanation, then the situation changed drastically.

But we have to be careful here. Explaining away the burglar does not automatically guarantee that no burglar existed. It is possible (although no doubt unlikely) that a burglar had snuck in and was just getting ready to steal your valuables when the cat knocked the textbooks onto the floor, thus making the noise you heard, and the burglar—suddenly alarmed— immediately snuck out of the house, leaving no traces, and went looking for a house to burgle where there were no interfering cats. But if your only evidence for a burglar was the noise you heard, if the only reason you had for believing in a burglar was that the presence of a burglar could initially explain the noises, then when you discover the better explanation, the initial explanation is explained away, and you no longer have any good reason to believe in the burglar. Continuing to believe in the burglar would, at that point, cease to be rational.

That sort of pattern is quite common in various academic disciplines. For instance, scientists no longer believe in things like phlogiston, caloric, and the quintessence, because the *only* reason those things were ever proposed was to explain such observed phenomena as combustion, heat flow, and stellar structures. When those explanations were superseded by better explanations (i.e., oxygen, molecular motion, and gravitational dynamics), continuing to believe in them was no longer rational. No one has ever proved that something like phlogiston might not exist in some remote, isolated corner of the cosmos, but we no longer have the slightest reason to believe that there is such a thing; our entire grounds for belief, the rationality of belief in phlogiston, has been removed by the explanation that explained it away.

Two conditions must be met if a case of explaining away is to remove the rationality of belief in something:

A. The thing in question must be genuinely explained away (F1–F3 must be met).
B. There must be *no other reason* for believing in the thing; that is, the only reason for belief must have been a now-debunked explanation.

It has become quite fashionable among religious critics to argue against the rationality of religious belief in exactly this fashion. In general, such arguments go like this. People believe in God in order to explain the existence of the cosmos, the apparent order in the cosmos, various patterns in historical events, our own existence, religious experiences, and so on. But now, the argument continues, we have scientific explanations that are vastly superior to the appeal to God as an explanatory hypotheses. Thus, God is explained away (F1–F3 are all met, it is claimed). And since, it is alleged, the *only* reason there ever was for believing in God was a primitive attempt to explain those things, continuing to believe in God is as groundless and irrational as continuing to believe in the burglar, holding on to the idea of aliens as crop circle artists, and espousing such archaic concepts as phlogiston and caloric. You will get a chance to think about this topic further in the exercises for this chapter.

VI. Summary and Conclusion

When confronted by a puzzling, perhaps troubling, or sometimes even a perfectly familiar and ordinary phenomenon (event, fact, truth), we are often curious, we want to know what accounts for it, we wonder *why*. As Aristotle observed, philosophy begins in such wonder. And for that matter, so does science. What we are seeking in such cases is an explanation—indeed, "explanation" is often defined simply as an answer to a *why* question. Explanations, be they of everyday common sense matters, historical events, roommate behavior, scientific observations, theoretical subatomic occurrences, or nearly anything else, have a common structure. Explanations typically include both some general law, rule, or pattern either in nature or in human behavior, plus a specification of background initial conditions. Those two constituents properly combined into an intelligible narrative not only provide us with an understanding of the phenomenon in question, but often even allow us to anticipate or predict phenomena of that specific type in the future.

Like arguments, some explanations are good, and some leave a lot to be desired. Explanations can be evaluated for their strength by reference to various criteria, generally thought to include plausibility, consistency, relevance, simplicity, and empirical accuracy. Competing explanations of the same phenomena can also be compared by reference to their performance under these criteria. But there are sometimes disagreements about the meanings of the evaluative criteria, their ranking, and their specific applications, and such disputes must be settled by argumentation. Arguments also come into play when there are disagreements about which explanation is better than its competitors. Arguments here typically involve inferences to the best explanation.

Explanations are part of the intellectual commerce of everyday life. All of us give them; all of us receive them from others. But not all of us engage in scientific explanation. Scientific explanations are generally subject to more rigorous methods; they involve the precise specification of laws and patterns; they frequently involve theories that pertain to large swaths of reality, both seen and unseen; they develop and are refined over time as a result of professional research, testing, and mutual criticism. Because scientific explanation and reasoning play such important roles in our culture, we devote a separate chapter to it in the pages that follow.

12.

Scientific Inference

"Seriously? You don't accept evolution despite the overwhelming scientific evidence?"

"But that's just it, Andrea. Evolution isn't *real* science. By definition, science is what can be *proven* from what we see and observe and measure and test and repeat. But evolution isn't based on observation. No human has ever seen a reptile evolve over millions of years into a bird or whatever. And it isn't repeatable. Evolution is just a theory, just speculation."

"Yeah," Melissa jumped in. "You liberals are always trying to ram your phony theories down everyone's throats as science—like global warming. Last February was the coldest ever here. That's all the disproof I need. I almost froze."

"René, you are such a hypocrite," Andrea retorted. "That antibiotic you took last week for your sinus infection—it was made of molecules you can't see, to fight small bugs you can't see. And you too, Melissa. I seem to recall you telling Vic to insist on a paternity test before admitting anything. When it serves your purposes you're both perfectly happy to accept science, which, you might notice, not only involves all kinds of things we can't see—like viruses and molecules and DNA and stuff—but also works. It connects to reality in a way nothing else does."

"That's not the same thing, Andrea, and you know it. Medical science and chemistry and atoms and things like that maybe involve things we can't see directly, but they all involve things going on *now*, things that can be studied and repeated, and predictions that can be tested right here and now. And you just admitted they work. They make predictions you can observe and that means they pass scientific testing. Incidentally,

Melissa, that's why global warming is real science. It *is* happening now. It can be measured. The only reason you deny it is that you don't want to have to give up your SUV." René got an astonished glare and disbelieving splutter from Melissa, but continued on unchecked. "And Andrea, that's why Intelligent Design is real science too, because it involves things we can observe and investigate and test here and now. We can *see* the amazing way the immune system works, we can *see* the way everything in the whole universe is designed and adjusted perfectly for life to exist, and things like that. That's what real science does. It's not just speculation about the past like evolution." René was OK with science, but not with theories parading as science.

"Oh come on. If we can have good indirect evidence for viruses we have just as good indirect evidence for evolutionary theory. Maybe even better: we're here, and evolution explains how we got here. We wouldn't be here if evolution wasn't true. Anyway, Intelligent Design real science? Everyone sees through that smokescreen. It doesn't explain anything at all. It's just a way for you creationists to smuggle your own religion about divine purpose and creation into the conversation. And whether religion is true or not, science by definition can't involve anything that isn't completely natural. Theology, divine purpose, supernatural activity—it's all untestable and unpredictable and can't be talked about in science. There's no room for that stuff in science. If you creationists are allowed to bring religion into your so-called science then the next thing you try will be to censor all references to evolution or anything else your religion disagrees with."

"Censorship? Now who's the hypocrite?" René shot back furiously. "You were the one who just issued the edict about what can't be even talked about in science. That, Andrea, is censorship, in case you can't recognize it when you yourself propose it."

"I don't believe it"—this from Melissa. "After last semester I thought I had escaped philosophy forever, and now both of you guys are squabbling about definitions? Science is about the real world. Definitions are just invented by humans. They're just made up. Definitions and philosophy stuff like that has nothing to do with anything real."

Andrea was peeved. "Oh really? And when you say that global warming isn't good science, that it's all a left-wing hoax? Exactly how do you propose to tell good science from phony science without some idea— some *definition*—of what science actually is? Or what something has to be in order to be real science? Like always, you're doing exactly the same things you get huffy about when someone else does them."

That evening, the three of them ate at separate tables in the dining hall.

I. Philosophy and Scientific Inference

In the foregoing conversation, we witnessed some sharp disagreements about specific scientific ideas. But the disagreements went deeper than just specific scientific ideas. The nature of scientific reasoning, the character of science itself, and the criteria for good science were in dispute as well.

Of course, philosophy itself does not generally employ scientific inferences. But science and its methods are relevant to philosophy. Here are just three ways.

First, the contents of science—both intellectual and practical—shape the *context* of contemporary intellectual life and everyday existence. Science shapes the worldview matrix, the thought patterns, within which we pursue philosophy. It thus indirectly affects the content of philosophy as well. Knowing something about the logical moves involved in producing the content of science is important in evaluating the legitimacy of the influences that permeate philosophy.

Second, science constitutes one of the most successful *epistemological* projects we humans have ever managed to pull off. Over the centuries science has increasingly learned how to address questions to nature and how to read nature's answers. In the process it has produced deep, reliable, and confirmable insights into broad areas of reality, insights that have been achieved by few other methods. Some philosophers (like John Locke) have even argued that philosophy could learn some valuable epistemological lessons from science. To the extent that science is a case of genuine knowledge acquisition, it is of interest to philosophers. Philosophers want to know how knowledge works.

Third, all the reasoning that we engage in is thoroughly *human* reasoning. We employ human concepts, human thought patterns, and human cognitive abilities. The scientific reasoning that we do thus often resembles and overlaps with various kinds of reasoning already discussed in this book—deductive, inductive, analogical, probabilistic, and explanatory. Since logic, the study of reasoning, is a basic component of philosophy, scientific reasoning is of interest to philosophers in its own right.

The unavoidable overlap between scientific inference and more general modes of human reasoning is in part why science in its methods has often been described (even by scientists) as "organized common sense." But the task of explicating science and the details of scientific inference beyond that informal characterization is complicated by the absence of any precise definition of science. There have been numerous definitions proposed over the past few centuries, but none has withstood detailed examination. Indeed, scientists themselves have fought over what science is, what constitutes proper scientific method, what types of inferences are scientifically legitimate, and what might distinguish good science from bad science, real science from pseudoscience.

This is not a chapter on the philosophy of science. But in tracking how the various forms of logic we've already studied function in science, we'll gain some insight into how science works. In what follows, we will explore some ideas about what science is and discuss some of the ways that logic has shaped various conceptions of scientific inference, scientific reasoning, and scientific method.

I. Deductivism

From ancient Greek times, and perhaps before, deductive reasoning—whether in the form of geometry, mathematics more generally, or deductive logic—has been held up as the paradigm of reasoning and rationality. Deductive reasoning promised absolute rigor, secure inferential paths, and invulnerable proofs. Done correctly, deduction removed the risk of going astray between premises and conclusion. Given secure premises—truths of reason, eternal conceptual truths, necessarily true axioms, and the like—the conclusions deduced from those premises could not possibly be in error. Remember: in valid deductive arguments, if the premises are true, the conclusion has to be true. Products of deduction with sturdy starting points were hallmarks of rationality, paradigms of real knowledge—not human opinion, hope, speculation, guesswork, blind faith, mere belief, or suspicion, but guaranteed you-bet-your-life-on-this knowledge.

This deductive pattern—with a couple crucial innovations—found early expression in Aristotle's conception of science. Many of Aristotle's contemporaries argued that real truth was found only in the transcendent, immaterial realm. The pure intellect, turning away from sense experience, reached transcendent axioms, and deduction took it from there. Knowledge was not to be found in the physical realm. Physical things contained no deep truths to be uncovered. But Aristotle saw things a bit differently. On his view, physical things in nature did in some sense embody truths, truths that could be discovered. And the process of discovery began not with sheer intellect but with sensory observation. Given just a few of the right kind of observations of natural objects or processes, the mind, through a process Aristotle called "induction" (*epagōgē*), could seize upon the universal principles embodied in those objects or processes. And those principles could then serve as the axioms from which other truths of nature—biological, astronomical, geological, and so forth, depending upon the area of investigation—could be deduced.

So we could have genuine knowledge not only of the things philosophers like to think about, like metaphysics, ethics, and logic, but also of physical things, material processes, biological organisms, and other constituents of nature. We could have knowledge of scientific matters. Still, all knowledge—whether of metaphysics, ethics, logic, astronomy, physics, or biology—consisted of a foundation of true fundamental principles (axioms grasped by the mind on the basis of sensory experience) plus whatever could be rigorously deduced from those axioms.

Centuries later, the **deductivist** idea of having watertight proofs concerning scientific matters through deduction looked very attractive to people such as Galileo (self-proclaimed last of the true Aristotelians) and Descartes (despite the fact that he had no use for Aristotle). There are even strong echoes of deductivism in the major works of influential scientists in the modern period (e.g., Isaac Newton's *Principia Mathematica*). Indeed, the perception that science is a matter of mathematical or logical deduction from utterly secure starting points and offers rigorous proofs is still very much with us. Statements about scientific proof are a standard fare in popular discourse, as are attempts to win arguments by claiming that science has "proven" this or that theory. Equally common are attempts to refute theories by asserting that they have not been scientifically proven. Proof —or disproof—is indeed a powerful intellectual key to truth, and the idea of proof has become a powerful rhetorical weapon in arguments about science.

Iᴀ. Cᴀᴜᴛɪᴏɴs: Fɪʀsᴛ Wᴀᴠᴇ

It is unfortunate that, given its attractions, the deductivist picture of science is defective in several significant ways. Later in this chapter it will become clear why the deductive inferences involved in science are far more complex than we might think. To begin with, we can point out two preliminary difficulties with deductivism.

First, we have come to realize that we have neither a logical procedure nor a mental faculty that can distill the essence, the underlying universal defining principles, or the ultimate constituents of the phenomenon in question from a few relatively ordinary observations. In some cases we do extract universals from a few particulars. For instance, we don't have to dissect very many cows before we grasp the fact that all cows have four stomachs. But in those cases the general insight we attain does not involve the kind of hidden, unobservable theoretical entities that play an essential role in science we know today. The concepts of, say, atoms, quarks, black holes, DNA, and the deep past are not results of a few quick observations of cows, rocks, stars, snowflakes, family resemblances, or gently rolling hills. They emerge as a result of a lot of hard thinking, gallons of coffee, carefully constructed experiments, theorizing, and a good deal of human creativity—sometimes even inspired genius.

Second, science does not produce proofs —either positive or negative—in any formally rigorous sense. The logic-based reasons for this claim will become clear a little later. Even Aristotle conceded that when deduction is applied to the natural realm, we only get truths "for the most part." The fit is inexact. Science is not absolutely infallible—any more than the humans who do science. Recognizing this point, science at its best is not dogmatic. There is always in principle a degree of tentativity in science. Its results are provisional. Science is always open, at least in principle, to new data, new interpretations, new insights, new discoveries, new theories, new questions. In fact, science exhibits a long history of discovering weaknesses in its own theories and having the integrity to replace them (sometimes after long and bitter struggles) with better ones. That historical pattern serves as a caution against hanging on to present scientific theories with a dogmatic grip as if they had been proven once and for all.

On the other hand, one should not fall into the opposite error and be overly skeptical about science. Most people, including practicing scientists, endorse a broad type of **scientific realism,** holding that one key goal of science is the discovery of truth and that science often succeeds in that quest. Despite the necessary tentativity of science, we often embrace specific results of science with a great deal of confidence. And sometimes that is exactly as it should be. Science is epistemically powerful. It confronts reality in ways unmatched by most other human epistemic endeavors. The fact that it does not produce formal, rigorous proofs and that it is always in principle possible for specific results and theories to be wrong, is by itself no justification for **scientific antirealism**—denying that science aims at, ever achieves, or can ever recognize truth in its theories. Much less does the absence of absolute proof in science constitute justification either for dismissing science or for failing to come to honest grips with theories one might abhor—whether that be evolution, Intelligent Design, climate change, or something else. Eventually the theories one opposes may indeed be shown to be mistaken. That is always a possibility. But one cannot responsibly pretend that they need not be taken seriously if they cannot be proven, or that their advocates can be dismissed as dishonest, deluded, stupid, or wicked because they have no complete proofs.

What is it, then, that makes for scientific knowledge if not deductive logic? One answer to this question—very general, but generally accepted—is that what counts as scientific are the results, principles, and theories that are the intellectual end products of a methodical, rigorous process of reasoning. But this general view still leaves unanswered the following questions:

A. What sort(s) of things should be taken as the *starting points* of scientific reasoning? The a priori truths of reason? Empirical observations?

And more central to our present focus:

B. What type(s*)* of *reasoning* should science follow? Deductive? Inductive? Both? Neither?

As you might expect, there have been many answers to these questions. We will briefly explore a few of the more prominent ones.

II. Inductivism

By the early modern period, many were convinced that reason alone could not provide reliable foundations for science. Uncontrolled, fanciful speculation was all too easy when reason was left to its own devices. There had to be some more solid, more constrained starting points free from potential human distortion. The answer: starting from what nature said, from the empirical observation of nature. But starting from a foundation of empirical observation, how was one supposed to proceed? How did one finally arrive at correct scientific general principles, at true scientific theories, at genuine scientific explanations? We don't have a reliable mental faculty that makes the leap automatically. And as it turned out, there is no deductive process that can properly take us from a collection of observational, empirical data either to (1) universal empirical principles of the sort science needs (e.g., that *all* planets *everywhere* for *all* times move in elliptical orbits) or to (2) principles involving unobserved theoretical objects and processes (e.g., electrons, quarks, events far in the past).

What, then, is the alternative? The **inductivist** idea was that one begins with proper observational evidence concerning whatever phenomenon one was scientifically investigating; then one applies strict inductive logic to that evidence, and the correct theory explaining that phenomenon would then result from that logic. So using the right set of inductive logical procedures, one could reason from the data to explanatory theory.

There were different views of precisely how that worked and what the proper inductive procedures involved. The most influential came from Francis Bacon in the early 1700s, often credited with first stating "the" scientific method. The inductivist pattern—going from observational, empirical evidence via various inductive procedures to theory—not only was historically influential but continues to be held today in many popular circles.

Empirical, observational evidence was taken to be completely objective, to be the voice of nature itself dictating information to us through the senses. Inductive logic, if applied correctly, would take us reliably from premises to conclusion, from input to output, or in this case from empirical data to scientific theory. Thus, this method would produce secure, reliable, and authoritative revelations of scientific truth. Such a method was to be especially valued because it was not only a powerful tool for revealing truth but also immune to distorting biases, presuppositions, philosophical commitments, religious blind spots, political agendas, and other subjective "impurities" that humans inject into intellectual endeavors. The "scientific method" was credited with having such immunity because it involved only observational data (what *nature*—not mere humans—said) and rigorous logic (what *reason*—not individual humans—judged to be the case). Neither component harbored a subjective taint; consequently, the results of the method did not either. Science was pure and objective, uncontaminated by humanity and its foibles.

IIA. CAUTIONS: SECOND WAVE

Attractive as that picture was, it did not work. No known form of logic (either inductive or deductive) can take one from a collection of empirical data (no matter how extensive) to a theory of that data. There is no process of logic by which empirical data can produce, generate, or create theories. That is why we can't look to brilliant logicians—such as your philosophy professors—for the next scientific breakthrough. Furthermore, no matter how large the data collection one has, there are always in principle infinitely many potential explanatory theories covering those data. The data do not nail down a unique theory. This fact, generally known as the *underdetermination of theory by empirical data*, has been recognized off and on since the 14th century. As we'll see, **underdetermination** has some important implications.

Some were tempted to argue that if theories could not be gotten from empirical data and logic alone, then science should dispense with theories, holding firmly to the purity of empirical data and whatever limited results logic could generate from the data. But that proposal didn't work either. The nature of science itself got in the way. Science trades in theories. Roughly speaking, in science a theory is a universal descriptive or explanatory account of some class of phenomena. For example, the heliocentric theory presented a description of the solar system (with the earth and other planets in motion around the sun). That theory not only explained various observed phenomena (e.g., planetary retrograde motion) better than had previous theories, it also provided the basis for predicting other observable phenomena (e.g., large fractional phases of Venus). The major functions of science—description, prediction, explanation—are all keyed to theory. And it is in terms of theories that science performs its most fundamental function: allowing us to understand phenomena in nature (e.g., why the outer planets move in retrograde fashion only at opposition).

A theory may be a very provisional guess. Or it may be extremely well confirmed. What defines a theory is not its level of confirmation. Heliocentric theory, gravitational theory, relativity theory, atomic theory, kinetic theory, and the biological theory of evolution are all well-confirmed theories that describe reality, explain phenomena, support predictions, and thus allow us to understand things in their respective domains. They are well confirmed, but they are still theories. What defines a theory is its structure and the role it is meant to play in scientific thinking. To reject or criticize a scientific theory on grounds that it is "only a theory" is thus to completely misunderstand the concept of theory as used in science.

Theories are essential to science. Science simply cannot function without them. But if logic and empirical data cannot in principle generate scientific theories, where do they come from? The answer, as it turns out, is the human imagination. Scientific theories are born of human creativity, human invention, human inspiration. But human creativity is not a rigorously governed process. It has no known rules, and it does not seem to follow any procedure (although many people believe that analogical thinking plays a role here). Who knows what may or may not trigger a leap of scientific imagination? The process is a thoroughly subjective one. But since science cannot operate without theories, those subjective processes are undeniably part of science. Thus the pressing question arises: Is there any way to allow theories into science, but to keep the human subjectivity of theory creation from infecting—and corrupting—the purity of science? Remember: it was that purity that was to give science its legitimacy and authority.

III. Hypothetico-Deductivism

The answer to that pressing question, popular for many decades, was the **hypothetico-deductive** method. The basic idea was that it didn't really matter where proposed theories came from, so long as nature itself had the final word on which proposals were allowed to become part of science. And nature gave that word empirically through the results of scientific testing. So any theory whatever could apply to get into science, but nature decided which applicants were admitted.

Here's how it was supposed to work. Something in nature interests or puzzles a scientist, who begins observing the phenomenon more carefully and collects some initial data concerning it. In light of this initial set of data, she by some process of creative insight (it doesn't matter what process) formulates a tentative hypothesis, a provisional theory, to account for the data. She then figures out what would happen in some as yet unexamined situation if the hypothesis were correct. That is, from the *hypothesis* she *deduces* a prediction (hence, the *hypothetico-deductive* method). She then tries to produce the new situation. She might set up an experiment, perhaps in a laboratory. Or maybe she has to wait for nature to set up the situation and then observes what happens. (Suppose that the theory is about supernovas. Supernovas cannot be set up in a laboratory at our convenience, so one waits and observes nature.) If the results predicted by the proposed theory actually occur, they're taken to count in favor of the theory. The theory tells us that some specific thing will happen, and nature says that the theory's prediction is right. Successful prediction was widely regarded as providing some support for the theory, or as constituting some degree of confirmation of the theory. If the predicted result does not occur, that is generally taken to count against the theory: the theory made a pronouncement and nature said that the theory just plain got it wrong. Unsuccessful prediction was widely taken as falsification of the theory.

IIIa. Cautions: Third Wave

At this point material in the chapter on deductive logic becomes relevant. But in perhaps unexpected ways. Notice that the basic structure of confirmation just outlined above is something like this: the scientist deduces that

> if the hypothesis being tested (H) is true,
> then we should observe the predicted result (R).

Then, when the scientist checks,

> we do observe the predicted result (R).

Therefore . . . Therefore what? If we say,

> Therefore the hypothesis being tested (H) is true,

then we have just committed the fallacy of affirming the consequent. But does science really rest on a simple invalid argument form? That sounds a bit worrisome. Of course, if we say only,

> Therefore the hypothesis being tested (H) is *probably* true,

we haven't made that simple deductive mistake. It is, however, difficult (indeed, often impossible) to say just how probable some specified collection of data and test results make the hypothesis in question. Nonetheless, it was widely held that making true predictions to some degree confirmed the hypothesis that made those predictions, and that the more—and more surprising—true predictions a hypothesis made the higher the degree of confirmation.

In any case, this type of confirmation never constitutes a proof, despite the fact that we frequently hear people say "science has proven" this or that theory. No matter how many correct predictions a theory or hypothesis makes, it is always at least possible that some future prediction will turn out to be mistaken, and on this view, that one incorrect prediction will show the theory to be false despite all the past true predictions. This is one reason why it is widely believed that scientific theories must always be held tentatively. The tentative attitude toward its own results is often cited as distinguishing science from religion, the latter often seen as dogmatic. The perceived tentativity of science and the associated willingness of science to change its positions in the face of new or contrary evidence is widely regarded as allowing science to correct itself, to abandon past mistakes and make continual progress—again in contrast to religion's alleged dogmatism and associated refusal to change its beliefs come what may. Critics often cite this stubborn attitude as the source of "intellectual stagnation" in religion.

But the idea of scientific confirmation seems problematic to some philosophers and scientists, especially in light of two problems: first, theory confirmation looks like the fallacy of affirming the consequent; second, there are the troubling implications of the underdetermination of theory by empirical data. In addition, there is the problem mentioned above of specifying the exact probabilities of theories on the available data. In fact, according to some, the problem is even worse than first thought. Scientific hypotheses and theories are typically universal. For instance, *all* electrons have a specific mass, *all* sharks have certain characteristics, and according to Newton *every* bit of matter attracts *every other* bit of matter in specifiable ways. But we have examined only a vanishingly small fraction of all the electrons in the universe, of all the sharks in the ocean, and of all the bits of matter in the universe. How does science get from the few observed cases to all cases? Does science routinely commit the fallacy of hasty generalization in order to get to its theories? That question leads to very complex issues—some even involving metaphysical presuppositions (such as the uniformity of nature).

A second and more radical worry is this. Given the universality of theories, a theory can produce an unlimited number of predictions. But at any given time only a finite number of those predictions has been checked. And given that any finite number of checked predictions is exactly zero percent of a theory's infinitely many possible predictions, the probability of a theory being true on the evidence of the actually confirmed predictions is also exactly zero. That means, some have argued, that there simply is no such thing as confirmation even if we have verified predictions.

But as we emphasized earlier, we should not lose sight of the fact that science in many instances succeeds in giving us genuine insights into the world around us; clearly it is one of the most powerful of human epistemic projects. And most scientists and philosophers continue to believe that theories receive a degree of confirmation from positive results in test situations. Granted, complexities and puzzles remain in understanding exactly how this works. Granted, caution and tentativity are called for. But wholesale skepticism, galloping relativism, and scientific antirealism are not warranted on the basis of the foregoing considerations. The problems we've identified may have more to do with a defect in our understanding of science than with a defect in science itself.

IV. Falsificationism

In light of the problems afflicting the hypothetico-deductive model of science, a number of philosophers and scientists abandoned the whole idea of confirmation, arguing that the real power of science lay not in establishing what is true, but in eliminating what is false. If science can't nail down the truth, it can at least uncover and learn from its own mistakes. This **falsificationist** view took the same view of empirical testing proposed in the hypothetico-deductive picture. But having rejected the concept of confirmation, it instead focuses on predictions that fail to be true. According to falsificationists, scientists generate a prediction from the hypothesis to be tested, just as they do in hypothetico-deductivism:

> If the hypothesis being tested (H) is true,
> then we should observe the predicted result (R).

The scientist then performs the experimental or observational test. If the predicted result occurs, that means only that the hypothesis has survived that particular test, not that it is confirmed or more likely to be true. The probability is still exactly zero. But on the other hand, suppose that

> we do not observe the predicted result (R).

One then concludes:

> Therefore, the hypothesis being tested (H) is false.

That conclusion seems logically impeccable. In fact, the inference is an instance of the deductively valid argument form modus tollens. Thus it looks like the logical propriety of science has been rescued. The falsificationist picture of scientific inference was developed and advocated by Karl Popper in the 1930s, and many scientists today identify themselves as Popperians or falsificationists.

IVA. CAUTIONS: FOURTH WAVE

But again, things aren't quite as simple as the model would have us believe. Hypotheses or theories taken by themselves do not generate predictions. Suppose that you are the first human to land on an alien planet. Seeing a good chance to lose your philosophy text and thereby not have to finish the reading for next week, you throw it away from you as hard as you can. But you wonder: How far away will the textbook land? To calculate that prediction, you would probably want to employ part of Newton's gravitational theory. But the theory alone doesn't generate an answer. To get the answer you have to add into the calculation the mass of the alien planet, the mass of the textbook (no doubt considerable), the angle of the throw, the acceleration of the throw, the curvature of the planet's surface, and a host of other such "initial" or "boundary" conditions. That means that generating even a simple prediction of how far your textbook will travel requires a theory or hypothesis (Newton's theory, in this case) *plus* other factors:

[Hypothesis (H) + boundary conditions (B)] →
predicted result (R)

But there's more. If you were doing an esoteric experiment involving, say, subatomic entities, you would be relying on some high-tech instruments and apparatus. And you would assume that they were functioning properly. You would also be depending upon the theories that went into their design and operation. And you would employ other theories in interpreting their outputs. In short, you would be employing a variety of "auxiliary" theories. So the prediction situation is more like this:

[Hypothesis (H) + boundary conditions (B) + auxiliary
theories (A)] → predicted result (R)

Now the testing situation gets really tricky. Suppose that the predicted result (R) turns out not to be correct. Modus tollens tells us that something has gone wrong. But the problem could involve (H) or (B) or (A). Maybe the theory you're testing is false. But maybe not—maybe the boundary condition were not specified accurately; maybe your instruments aren't working properly; or maybe you're not interpreting the outputs of the instruments correctly. Or maybe the prediction failed because of some combination of these problems. Modus tollens does not tell us which one is the problem. Of course we try to accurately specify boundary conditions, and we try to employ only true auxiliary theories in our derivations of the predictions and the interpretation of the test results. But remember that theories (including the auxiliary theories we assume to be true) are never actually proved to be true. So there is always a chance one or more of them is not correct. And although we need not go into all the details here, there are in fact many more components to any derivation than just boundary conditions and auxiliary theories. Each one of those additional components further complicates the test situation. Some of them even involve presuppositions concerning the recognition and classification of empirical data themselves. Empirical data are not just a matter of nature dictating information to us via the senses. We have to conceptualize them first.

Thus not only can theories not be rigorously proven *true* purely on the basis of empirical data, but they generally cannot even be rigorously proven *false* purely on the basis of empirical data either. Beyond that, the underdetermination of theory by empirical data makes clear that no amount of empirical data and logic can ever single out or point toward some one particular theory as the right one. But scientists often do accept some single theory as the correct one—relativity theory, for example—despite the logical problems with confirmation, the problems with probabilities, the problems with both empirical proof and falsification, and the implications of the underdetermination of theory by empirical data. So on what basis do scientists select a single theory as the right theory, as the best explanation?

V. A Values-Shaped Picture

Most philosophers of science as well as many scientists now recognize that empirical considerations plus logic are by themselves simply incapable of accounting for science as we actually pursue it. There are in fact several broader considerations that operate within science as part of the basis for the selection and acceptance of theories. For example, other things being equal, a theory that is empirically accurate is considered to be better than one that is less accurate. A theory that fits well with already-accepted scientific theories is preferred to one that is in tension with them. A theory that applies across a broad range of phenomena is preferred to one limited to only one small area. A theory that generates new, novel predictions is preferred to one that does not. And many scientists take a theory that is simpler to be better than a needlessly complicated theory.

There is no complete and agreed-upon list of such criteria. In fact they are the subject of frequent dispute even among scientists themselves, and the generally accepted list has changed repeatedly throughout the history of science. But among the most influential criteria are

- empirical accuracy;
- empirical breadth;
- explanatory power;
- consistency with other scientific theories;
- consistency with other deeper (e.g., metaphysical, philosophical) principles;
- fruitfulness in suggesting new lines of investigation and new research questions;
- predictive power; and
- simplicity, mathematical elegance.

Some related criteria were also briefly mentioned in the earlier chapter on explanation.

Most scientists also take as nonnegotiable the criterion that legitimate scientific theories deal only with natural entities, processes, and events (**methodological naturalism**), whether or not a nonnatural or supernatural realm exists. That criterion has been hotly disputed by some creationists and some (but not all) advocates of Intelligent Design, who argue (as even some scientists have said) that science is an attempt to get at truth "no holds barred."

Again, the above list is neither complete nor uncontroversial. But theories that do well on those criteria are taken to be better than those that don't, and scientists generally favor theories that exhibit such properties.

Va. Cautions: Fifth Wave

There are important things to note here. First, the criteria listed above come in degrees. Theories can be more or less broad, more or less simple, more or less explanatorily powerful. Second, the criteria can conflict with each other. Theories typically do not do equally well on all criteria. One theory may do a better job of explaining something while a competing theory is a bit more accurate. Those conflicts can lead to some serious scientific disagreements. Third, criteria can be ranked differently. When two criteria conflict, scientists can (and do) disagree over which of the two criteria is most important, which should outweigh the other. Which theory is better: the one that is slightly more accurate, or the one that explains better? Which theory is better: one that can be applied a bit more broadly, or one that is mathematically a little cleaner? There have been numerous disagreements among scientists over such questions in specific cases.

Fourth, note that none of the questions that arise concerning the ranking of such criteria can be settled empirically. There is simply nothing that could show up in the bottom of a test tube, on an astronomical photographic plate, in a laboratory dissection, or in an accelerator readout that would indicate that accuracy is a greater virtue in a theory than consistency with other theories a scientist already accepts. That is a decision for scientists to make. When a scientist says that a mathematically elegant theory is better than a mathematically messy one, or when a scientist says that theoretical explanatory power is more important than theoretical fruitfulness, she is making a value judgment. The criteria function as values in the scientific context, and selection of a single "best" theory from among competing theories more closely resembles a value decision than a purely logical inference. (This point is directly linked to inference to the best explanation, discussed in the chapter on explanation.) A scientist's value judgments may be exactly right. But the fact still remains that it is a human judgment—not a simple empirical result, not a direct pronouncement of nature itself, not the dictate of logic alone.

But most, if not all, scientists and philosophers of science agree that science is after the sober truth, not just what conforms to their preferences. If empirical data plus logic are insufficient to get us there, then other things—such as normative criteria for theories—*have* to be brought into the process. Since nature does not tell us what those criteria should be, on what basis should we decide what criteria and values to bring in? The reason most scientists recognize specific value criteria is because they think those values are potential marks of truth in a theory. For instance, other things being equal, a simple theory is widely thought to be more likely to be true than a more complicated theory. Since these criteria function as provisional guides to truth, they are often referred to as **epistemic values**.

There is a deeper lesson here as well. Why would one take, say, mathematical elegance to point toward scientific truth? As most scientists see it, for a theory to be true it must in some way reflect reality itself. Thus, to accept mathematical elegance as an epistemic value is in effect to accept the metaphysical assumption that reality, at root, is mathematically elegant. In fact, adopting any epistemic value as a criterion for evaluating scientific theories is to accept a corresponding metaphysical presupposition. And doing that puts metaphysical presuppositions squarely at the heart of the scientific enterprise. Many would like to keep metaphysics out of science. But as we've seen, there simply is no way to avoid using value criteria within science. Logical problems with the confirmation and falsification of theories, the underdetermination of theories by empirical data, and like considerations, mean that if science is attempting to get at truth, it will have to employ a collection of values as nonempirical criteria, and those values cannot be taken as epistemic values without corresponding metaphysical underpinnings.

Given that the criteria for theory selection reflect human value judgments, and given the complexities of human sensory observation, some (perhaps most influentially Thomas Kuhn) have been led to adopt some form of scientific antirealism. They have concluded that getting at objective truth is simply beyond the reach of human science. Others (including various postmodernists) have claimed that the above considerations lead to a thoroughgoing relativism. But if the relevant scientific epistemic values are in sync with reality, if they reflect deep metaphysical truths—whether they arose through evolutionary processes, resulted from the divine creation of the human mind, or whatever—then neither antirealism nor relativism automatically follow from the human factors involved in science.

Do those epistemic values actually reflect deep metaphysical truths? Do they make for a match with reality? This is not the place to pursue the metaphysical underpinnings of science, their origins, or their justification. You can sign up for a philosophy of science class for that. But it is worth noting that most of the major early modern scientists (e.g., Galileo, Kepler, Newton, Boyle, Maxwell, and Pasteur) explicitly justified the metaphysical assumptions of their scientific work by reference to the doctrine of creation, where the idea of the uniformity of nature, for instance, was justified by reference to God's consistent faithfulness. After Darwin, others have suggested that evolutionary theory provides us with a justification for the assumption that our epistemic values and their metaphysical correlates track the truth. Others disagree, arguing that evolution selects most directly for the survival value of behavior, not the truth of beliefs.

VI. Summary and Conclusion

There is no single, unique mode of reasoning that only scientists engage in. The reasoning that science embodies consists of various types of logic already discussed in other chapters: deductive, inductive, probabilistic, analogical, and explanatory. Nearly all humans explicitly or implicitly employ all of those forms of reasoning in meeting the demands of both intellectual and everyday life. And nearly all of us (including scientists) manage to commit quite a few of the fallacies discussed in this book as well.

Many popular views about science turn out to be mistaken on closer examination. Theories cannot be deduced from facts. Experimental results do not prove theories. Experimental results do not conclusively disprove theories. Science is not value-free. And contrary to those who would like to view science as a strictly objective affair, science is not disconnected from deeply human themes—from value decisions, metaphysical assumptions, and perhaps even religious commitments.

None of the foregoing considerations mean that science is unreliable, or that it is not a powerful tool for getting at truth, or that it is not rationally justifiable, or that it should be rejected, or that it can safely be ignored. Indeed, none of those things is true. But they do mean that understanding how science works, why it is rationally legitimate, what its capabilities and limits are, and how it should be related to the wider network of belief are vastly more complicated than realized in popular perception (including the perception of religious, nonreligious, and anti-religious communities). Given the influential role science plays in our practical, political, intellectual, philosophical, and even religious lives, we would do well to understand science aright—not only the scientific theories we discuss, but how scientific reasoning actually works. Those whose beliefs about science or specific scientific theories (whether climate change, evolution, historical geology, or whatever) come from TV news sound bites, radio talk show hosts, religious commentators pontificating well beyond their expertise, atheist rants, or Saturday seminars in a church basement are nearly guaranteed to have a distorted, oversimplified, and largely inaccurate picture of the science in question. That is not to say that all scientific theories are right. But misrepresenting them (making them into straw men) certainly isn't right. In the chapter on the ethics of reasoning, we stress the importance of getting an accurate and adequate view of a position, even if we disagree with it.

And finally, in the case of science, following the threads of reasoning almost inevitably leads, as it does in other areas of human endeavor, deep into philosophy—which, fortunately, is where your class will go as well.

13.

The Ethics of Argument

The Hunger Games: challenging and thought provoking for 13-year-olds, or too disturbing in its depiction of violence? *Huckleberry Finn*: to be promoted as an American classic, or shunned for its use of the *n*-word? Many books (and films) are controversial, and for many different reasons. When J. K. Rowling's Harry Potter books first came out, some religious communities were worried because the books' heroes spent their teen years training their occult powers. Arguments ensued. Heated blogs flamed up on the Internet. Letters to the editor hit the published page, arguing both for and against. Take these two examples from *Christianity Today* (March 6, 2000, p. 10) a periodical serving the American evangelical community:

> The fact that Harry Potter engages in acts of "compassion, loyalty, and courage" . . . only confuses the moral compass of young readers. Witchcraft is the pursuit and use of power—without the blessing of God. That is why sorcerers are condemned by name in the book of Revelation, along with the sexually immoral and those who murder and deceive (Rev. 22:15). How can you deem Potter's involvement in witchcraft insignificant?

> An irony peculiar to the juvenile book field is that few adults—Christian or not, parents or not—will condescend to read children's books, while many of the same feel qualified to pass judgment on them. Rowling's story . . . is an

epic novel of good versus evil, where the heroes require help beyond natural strength and where good wins out. Are Hogwarts's witches more sinister than Oz's? Than Mary Poppins? It would be refreshing if Christians would look up from the pulp fiction and animated videos long enough to educate themselves in the field of literature, so they might think through and discuss its complexities and themes as ably as the world does.

Whatever side of this particular debate you might be inclined to agree with, and whatever you think about the arguments and their logical merits, there are further questions to ask about these pieces of reasoning. For example, how will each letter writer's tone come across to his or her audience? Are they inviting others to further dialogue and debate, and appealing persuasively to those who disagree? Or are they condescending to anyone not already in their camp, more interested in lobbing grenades than hearing a response? If you were the one they were addressing in debate, would you feel as if you were being addressed with respect, or would you feel the bite of their saintly superiority or their snarky sarcasm?

Plenty of things can go wrong in an argument, but only some of them have to do with the rules of logic. Being good at reasoning depends in part on being good at seeing the logical relations between propositions. But part of arguing well also involves being good to the people with whom one has a difference of opinion. And part of it is a matter of having the right purposes in argument, because these shape the practices we engage in and the way we characterize the positions of those who test—and sometimes detest—our point of view.

These sorts of concerns aren't usually addressed in logic textbooks. Traditionally they have been associated with the discipline of rhetoric, which deals with speaker-audience relations and the art of persuasion. More recently many would assign them to the category of discourse ethics. Both differ from logic. But when it comes to good human communication, they are just as important for reasoning well with others as constructing strong arguments and identifying logical fallacies.

I. Purpose

The word **philosophy** means the love of wisdom. But in the midst of doing philosophy it's easy to lose track of that original idea. Busy in critically assessing the views of others and responding to criticism of our own views, we often slide into the conviction that the main point of reasoning with others is personal vindication. The aim is to prove that we were right all along and that others, in daring to oppose us, are just plain wrong. We might even take some satisfaction in sharing an explanation of their error: they are wrong because they are ignorant, or arrogant, or gullible, or ill-intentioned, or intellectually sloppy, or in some other way substandard.

Here we want to remind ourselves of the primary purpose of reasoning with others and testing proposed arguments: the desire for truth and understanding. Wisdom is something we may have in part. But in many areas we remain properly perplexed; in other areas we may be quite sure of ourselves but entirely wrong. Reviewing reasons and evaluating arguments is one way to correct our errors and to acquire a deeper and more complete understanding of ourselves and the world around us. It's all about acquiring wisdom.

Even Socrates had to remind himself of this point. In his last conversation with his followers, as he awaited execution, he admitted that he was in danger of adopting a non-wisdom-loving attitude toward argumentation. Winning the argument was beginning to look more important to him than winning the truth. But if all he wanted was to get the better of his conversation partners, by his own admission he would be falling in with the "uneducated," who "give no thought to the truth about the subject of discussion but are only eager that those present will accept the position they have set forth" (*Phaedo*, 91a). He would recover the wisdom-loving attitude if he were eager only to use arguments to find out what is true, and only then eager to find others in agreement with him.

How do arguments help us in this project? Getting to wisdom usually requires some proverbial "iron sharpening iron"—that is, the thorough and rigorous assessment of arguments in dialogue with others. Philosophy is best done in community. We need conversation partners, even those who disagree with us. The mutual sharpening process that plays out in discussion and debate can yield better understanding for everyone involved. And because wisdom, unlike dessert, is a good that can be shared without reducing anyone's portion of it, wisdom-seeking can be a win-win proposition. It need not be a zero-sum game.

If that seems obvious upon reflection, consider the way the evaluation of arguments is often conducted: in attack mode. The usual metaphors are telling. They are typically combative, competitive, destructive, and violent:

- "I just shot that argument down in flames."
- "In my criticism I will attack the second premise."
- "This epistemic defeater trumps your prima facie case."
- "My opponent's position has thus been decimated."
- "By the time they were done debating, there was blood on the floor."

On this combative paradigm, argumentation is competitive. When someone wins, someone else loses. And while competition can bring out the best in us, too often the purpose on this paradigm is personal vindication and the enhancement of one's reputation for its own sake. Finding wisdom in a community of inquiry takes a backseat to coming out number one in the public eye. The goal of winning the truth is soon replaced by the goal of just winning.

Paul Griffiths, in a little book entitled *The Vice of Curiosity* on the virtues and vices of knowledge-seeking, describes a view of knowledge that is aimed at domination, mastery, and ownership. Here "knowledge is power"—power over our world, power over others, power to get our own way. Knowledge is something we achieve and wield to our own advantage. By way of contrast, the early medieval philosopher, Saint Augustine, put forward the view that knowledge is best seen as a gift. Such a view of our intellectual life yields an attitude of humility, gratitude, and good stewardship of what we know and the intellectual gifts by which we come to know it. Of course there may be other ways to achieve such intellectual virtues, but the contrast should be clear.

To test the nobility of your purposes in argument, rate what would give you more pleasure in a debate with your roommate:

- Knowing you are right.
- Shooting down all your roommate's objections to your view.
- Shooting them down with an audience of everyone within earshot.
- Having your roommate admit you are right, out loud, in front of said audience.
- Watching your roommate take notes on everything you say for the rest of the semester because everyone in your dorm now acknowledges you as their intellectual superior.
- Having a video of your intellectual triumph go viral on YouTube.
- All of the above.

Sure, it's satisfying to be right, or at least to be on the winning side of a dispute. And we all know how painful it feels to find out you're wrong about something. It can be even more painful to find that out in front of others and to have to admit your mistake publicly. And that's not always just because we think we're such intellectual hotshots and want a glorious reputation for our mental abilities. When an issue is really important to us, the stakes can be pretty high. Or if we've put a lot of work into crafting an argument, it can be hard to admit in the end that it doesn't work. This can make learning to do philosophy well in a classroom setting tough and risky work. But here's the deal: if we want to get things right (or somewhat closer to right), we will often need to make our views and supporting arguments vulnerable to the critical assessment of others.

Take the student who refused to let her father—a philosophy professor and logic whiz—read her papers before she turned them in. She preferred to avoid getting his comments because she knew they would require her to do more work revising her arguments. Worse yet, what if he found a major flaw in her paper and she couldn't figure out how to correct it before the deadline? Sure, it felt better to avoid finding out what was wrong with the paper; and it was definitely easier not to have to spend another two hours fixing her mistakes. But that turned out to be a great way to get Bs on her papers instead of As. More importantly, it was a great way of settling for something less than the wisdom she was capable of acquiring.

In the classroom, in the dorms, on the Internet, or around the dining table, consider how the discussion of controversial topics often goes. These exchanges often degenerate into exercises in disrespect, mutual incomprehension, and intimidating displays of intellectual one-upmanship. Positions are misrepresented, persons are attacked, motives are impugned, views are caricatured with loaded words. The conflict takes off under full steam while the common search for truth gets left in the dust.

If that scenario seems completely unfamiliar to you, be thankful that you dwell in a bright, cheerful, and supportive peer group. Communities of inquiry can operate on different principles. Things look refreshingly different when discussion partners gather for the purpose of supporting each other in the search for truth by hearing each other out and offering constructive criticism; when the main goal is not to win at all costs, but to grow in understanding; when they take each other as trusted partners, not adversaries; when they could even feel comfortable responding to a question by saying, "I don't know the answer to that; I'll think about it."

In such a setting, would going public with your opinions and reasons still be difficult and intimidating at times? Probably. Would there still be disagreement? Hard to avoid that in any group of human beings! But would the tone and outcome be different for all involved? You bet.

II. People

If our purpose is to learn and to discover something more of the truth, then the way we treat the people we argue with and the positions they hold should reflect that purpose.

In discussion and debate, scholars often refer to **the principle of charity**. When you hear that expression in an academic setting, you might think it means giving your loose change to desperately poor college students. Not a bad guess, but that's a different kind of charity. In its usage among academics—who have already spent all their loose change on books anyway—this principle says, in effect, "Treat your partner in dialogue and her arguments as you would want you and your arguments to be treated." It's the Golden Rule applied to discourse ethics. Philosopher Nicholas Wolterstorff memorably put the point in negative form as a commandment for all those involved in scholarship: "Thou must not take cheap shots."

In an article that appeared in the June/July 1999 issue of the *Cresset*, Wolterstorff explains the commandment this way,

> If [we are] going to engage in that practice of our common humanity which is called scholarship, then [we are] thereby under obligation to honor [our] fellow participants by understanding as well as [we] can how [others] are thinking and where, to put it colloquially, they are "coming from."
>
> Thou must not take cheap shots. Thou must not sit in judgment until thou hast done thy best to understand. Thou must earn thy right to disagree. Thou must conduct thyself as if Plato or Augustine, Clement or Tertullian, were sitting across the table—the point being that it is much more difficult (I don't say impossible) to dishonor someone to his [or her] face. . . .

Such principles connect our purpose in reasoning to the people we are reasoning with and the positions they hold. Are we being respectful

to those who hold a position other than our own? Such respect can motivate us to represent and address their point of view more fairly. And
such respect can reflect our deeper purpose: to understand the truth of
the matter before us with the help of others. That may mean admitting
our own views might need revising, even just a little teeny tiny bit. We
risk missing genuine opportunities to gain wisdom when we dismiss the
arguments of others too hastily or expend all our energy on just defending our initial position.

Sometimes we are overly dismissive or arrogant in our attitude toward
those who disagree with us. In effect, we're saying: "You're such an idiot!
I'm not even going to bother with what you have to say!" Wolterstorff
once commented that one reason people do so much yelling in public
discourse and arguments over social issues is because they gave their
reasons in a calm tone of voice at first, but no one listened to them or
took them seriously. Their shrill tones of protest were prompted by the
dismissive attitudes of their opponents. What did these people really
want? It's what all of us want: to be heard and understood. To be granted
a fair hearing is to be treated with dignity.

To break the cycle of callous disrespect and shrill protest, we ought
to start out by respecting others as reasoners—that is, as people capable
of offering legitimate reasons for their views. If we come to believe that
people are arguing in bad faith, that should be a conclusion drawn from
some hefty evidence, not an assumption we bring to the debate. When
we treat others with contempt and slap a snarky label on their position,
we are not only failing to be good truth-seekers, we're treating others
poorly. This is perhaps easier to do with historical figures or over the
Internet than it is with people we are talking to face-to-face. But it can be
a problem in any context. Treating others with ridicule and disrespect is
an excellent strategy only for those human beings who have nothing left
to learn about anything from anyone. Which leaves the rest of us.

Consider these examples, two from face-to-face interactions and two
from student papers:

> John stood in front of the school gym, representing the board
> of a private, church-related school. He gave a presentation
> on the pros and cons of placing a cell phone tower on the
> corner of the school campus, explaining the income gener-
> ated for the school and noting that safety concerns had been
> carefully considered. When he finished, Sharon stepped
> up to the microphone. "I can't believe you call yourself a

Christian," she said accusingly, "when you insist on exposing our precious children to dangerous radiation every day on the playground. All you businesspeople care about is the bottom line!"

Anna offered an argument against evolutionary naturalism, laying out reasons to think that it was reasonable to believe that God was behind evolutionary processes. Her opponent, Stephen, replied in a patronizing tone that anyone who believed in God these days was like a child who still who believed in the tooth fairy. It was time to grow up and accept the clear findings of scientific evidence. There was loud applause from the audience. Anna asked him which premise of her argument he found problematic. He snorted: "I'm not going to argue with someone who believes in fairy tales! Go on and be deluded—it's a free country."

"Plato's views about art and music in the *Republic* are obviously misguided. It's difficult to believe he was serious. Anyone who knows anything about culture knows that the freedom to be creative and express yourself are important and that censorship just leads to totalitarianism."

"It's a waste of time to read Descartes's arguments about the nature of the human mind. His view of consciousness is so antiquated; we all know that his view of the pineal gland as the point of connection between the mind and the body is a silly fiction. Psychology and cognitive science can tell us all we need to know about the mind and they make these old philosophical theories totally obsolete."

These examples involve informal fallacies covered in an earlier chapter (most obviously, ad hominems, straw persons, loaded words, and appeals to the gallery). But they also express an attitude that says, "If you disagree with me, I'm going to assume the worst about you. I'm going to treat you as if you were intellectually deficient, or a person with terrible motives—at any rate, as a person not worth taking seriously at all." Behind the cases where reasoning with others goes off the tracks, there sometimes lies a moral failure that runs deeper than any logical mistake. Here the principle of charity serves as a corrective. It tells us to treat people the way we'd like to be treated; to talk to them the way we'd want to be talked to; to respect them just as we'd want to be respected.

If we are going to be wisdom lovers—not to mention good conversation partners and roommates that others can stand to live with—our aim will extend beyond just offering airtight reasons for things we already believe or stunning critiques of the things other people believe. How we treat other people matters, too. As difficult as it might be in practice, the charitable approach is a win-win for all involved. If you are a fruitful conversation partner, other people will want to join you in conversation, and you're all likely to learn something.

III. Positions

We mentioned not one but two things that deserve your respect: first, your discussion partner. Second, your discussion partner's position. Take your roommate, for example, who thinks you are dabbling in the occult because he found a copy of the *Harry Potter and the Philosopher's Stone* under your pillow. His position will include two distinct things: the conclusion and the reasons offered for it. And they can be separated. He might be more attached to his conclusion than any reasons he has for it. In fact, he might be happy to switch his reasons halfway through the argument, if need be, rather than give up his conclusion. You are, after all, wearing that maroon-and-gold scarf a lot. But even if you ditch the scarf because your girlfriend says it's tacky, he doesn't let you off the hook. Even if you insist that chanting spells like "Expelliarmus!" helps you remember your Latin better than flashcards ever could, he'll reject that as a thin excuse if ever he's heard one. Of course, you don't have to like your discussion partner's position (the conclusion of his argument); you don't have to like the reasons he gives for it (the premises of the argument). In fact, you don't even have to like him. But you do have to be fair and consider them all in the best possible light.

Here's another word from Wolterstorff about how the sympathetic interpretation of another person's position is supposed to work,

> Genuine engagement entails both an effort to internalize the arguments of opposing viewpoints, understanding them from the inside, and an effort to examine one's own position from the outside, testing it for weaknesses. (These two necessary steps are represented, for example, in the Scholastic

method of *disputatio*, as practiced by Aquinas.) . . . One way to put it would be to say that many arguments are deeply flawed by a lack of imagination—imagination that allows a person to step outside herself, so to speak.

In other words, we owe it to the people we argue with to take their reasons seriously. Cases where we don't should be the result of careful and sympathetic consideration. We should not oversimplify their arguments (another informal fallacy) so that we are excused from giving their view a fair and thorough response. For this reason, we should not dismiss Plato's ethics in the *Republic* because we think he said something misogynist in Book V. Things are usually much more complicated than that. Maybe Plato's claims are ironic, or spoken by a character he expects the reader to disagree with; maybe the overall view is more respectful toward women than that single claim would suggest; or maybe not. Nonetheless, his views may be based on more complex and context-sensitive grounds that you need to find out about. Whatever conclusions we draw should rest on a fair interpretation of what Plato's position actually is. When it comes to historical figures, it's always a good idea to read texts holistically and to consider what might motivate someone in that time and place to hold such a view.

Richard Mouw has a little book on civil discourse called *Uncommon Decency*. In it, he notes that being civil to those we argue with—whether in politics or in the media or in a congregational meeting at a place of worship—should be part of the ground rules of debate. But unfortunately, civility is all too rare. We've been raised on the TV sitcom put-down and on smear-tactic political discourse. To be decent to those you argue with and their positions is consequently as uncommon as it is necessary.

So far we've set some lofty goals for ourselves: having a noble purpose, treating persons respectfully and charitably, and taking their positions seriously enough to engage them with integrity. How do we put these things into practice?

Here is a set of steps to help walk you through the process of responding to others in ways that make for productive discussion and debate:

1. Try to imagine your opponent's position and what might plausibly motivate it. Here are some questions you could ask yourself:

- What are the best sorts of reasons that might lead a person to hold such a view?

- If you had to defend such a view, what sorts of reasons would you offer for it?
- Can you sort or rank the reasons for such a view (both given and imagined) from best to least compelling?
- What commitments or values make it hard for you to sympathize with the view?
- What background commitments, values, or life experiences would make this view seem right to those who disagree with you?
- If we can't reach agreement, what would it look like to respectfully disagree?

2. Watch out for these frequent mistakes (note the overlap here with many informal fallacies):

- Name-calling and psychologizing (ad hominems). We could also call this "labeling and lumping." We declare our opponents guilty by associating them with a certain camp. Example:
  "The problem is that Republicans began telling folks what they truly believe. The GOP clown circus during the debates—with one unelectable GOP zealot after another, along with the audience itself and their heartless reactions—convinced most thinking and caring Americans that the GOP is a party of hate and division. Too late, GOP—your true colors have appeared."

- Oversimplifying (straw man, false dichotomy):
  "If you don't value protecting the lives of innocent children, go ahead and spend the big bucks on a stash of semi-automatic assault rifles. Is an assault on an innocent victim really a price you want to pay to keep the government from assaulting your Second Amendment right to bear arms?"

- Using inflammatory rhetoric to manipulate the conversation emotionally (loaded words, appeals to the gallery):
  "The proponents of abortion are so rabidly antilife that they would rather slay an innocent baby in cold blood than inhibit a woman's freedom to choose her own lifestyle."

"The president's health care plan is nothing but an under-handed endorsement of socialism, and no one commit-ted to the democratic values upheld by this great country should accept it."

Name-calling, oversimplifying, and emotionally manipulating the conversation constitute some of the ways of not taking others seriously and creating a shallow substitute for their real positions and the reasons they might have for them. What would it look like if we did try to honor others by engaging their actual position? People who support various political freedoms, and others who think those freedoms should be regu-lated, are not necessarily objecting to opposing views out of rank self-interest. Just because people disagree with us about moral or political issues doesn't mean that they are happy to endorse murder or seek the downfall of democracy. These caricatures and exaggerations are often an attempt to avoid serious argument altogether. When we resort to them, we seem intent on ignoring the real reasons people might have for hold-ing a view that differs from our own.

If your opponent is dishing out cheap shots, you are wise not to re-spond in kind. But let's be honest: this is a tough temptation to resist. Instead, refocus the conversation on the issue or disagreement at hand. What are the arguments for and against? What are the premises, both stated and unstated? Do the premises actually support the proposed con-clusion? The hardest thing to do in an argument is to separate criticism of the argument from criticism of the person offering it. Argumentation in the search for truth and understanding should focus on the criticism of arguments, not the criticism of persons.

If you can learn to show respect for others and interpret their posi-tions sympathetically, you will not only be an ethical reasoner in your philosophy class. You will also be better off in personal relationships, political discussions, and cultural debates. You will write better blogs and letters to the editor. And you'll be able to formulate and defend good policies on disputed issues at work without making it personal—and oth-ers will be more likely to listen to your views. You will be more likely to convince than alienate your audience. Here, as in other areas of life, do-ing the right thing is also a matter of doing the wise thing.

IV. Propensities: A Word about Character

So far we've put the basics of ethical reasoning in terms of rules and principles. There's another helpful way to look at the matter: What sort of people are we trying to be? What kinds of practices cultivate the character we'd like to see in ourselves? What kinds of attitudes and propensities constitute that character?

Anselm of Canterbury, a medieval thinker, began his most famous philosophical treatise, *The Proslogion*, with this prayer:

> Lord, I acknowledge and I thank you that you have created me in this your image, in order that I may be mindful of you, may conceive of you, and love you; but that image has been so consumed and wasted away by vices, and obscured by the smoke of wrong-doing, that it cannot achieve that for which it was made, except you renew it, and create it anew.
>
> I do not endeavor, O Lord, to penetrate your sublimity, for in no wise do I compare my understanding with that; but I long to understand in some degree your truth, which my heart believes and loves.

Note the combination of humility and confidence in this prayer. Anselm is painfully aware of his own cognitive limitations, and yet he expects to make real progress in his pursuit of knowledge. Anselm's prayer illustrates that both great and small efforts in the pursuit of truth can be motivated by a confidence that the project is not an exercise in futility, and yet acknowledge at the same time that, as Hugh of Saint Victor has said, "humility is required for study."

To achieve the right combination of humility and confidence when engaging in reasoning and argument, try assuming the posture of a lifelong learner, someone who does not yet have a complete and final view on every matter. This is especially helpful if you are engaging the view of a great mind in the history of ideas, like Plato, Augustine, Kant, Nietzsche, or Hannah Arendt. Think about your philosophical progress toward greater wisdom and insight as one of continuous upward leveraging: if you are willing to learn something in dialogue with others, then you have something to share with others who are still learning. But sharing what you've learned (or think you've learned) with a new or different audience raises new questions and additional challenges. Then you need to be willing to work on those issues and receive more feedback, which leads again to a new horizon of questions. And so on.

If you already think you're right and can't possibly be wrong, then you have nothing to learn and nowhere to grow. You've cut off the conversation before it can even get started. Even if you do have things right and you don't change your mind about your conclusions or commitments, you still have something to learn from the conversation. For example, you might learn how to respond better to objections (or anticipate potential objections); you might learn how to state your position with more precision and nuance; you might learn how to offer a more persuasive case to those who are skeptical or coming from a certain point of view; and you might learn of plausible reasons for positions you still disagree with so that you are less tempted to caricature or dismiss them in the future.

The right stance in these matters involves a delicate balance between too much and too little. Achieving it takes experience and some finely tuned discernment. The chart below is meant to illustrate a range of possible positions, following Aristotle's idea that for every virtue there is a vice of excess on one side and a vice of deficiency on the other.

Vice of Excess	Virtue	Vice of Deficiency
Arrogance, Obstinacy	*Epistemic humility plus Intellectual courage*	*Fearfulness, Lack of confidence*
Being overconfident about your access to truth or the rightness of your position or the nobility of your reasons.	Being appropriately confident about the things that deserve your confidence but also willing to listen to and learn from others when appropriate.	Not being confident enough of your position or reasons.
Being inflexible about your convictions.	Firmness combined with flexibility—reflecting the belief that some things are worth defending and yet their defenders are finite and fallible.	Not holding on to a position worth defending; being too flexible; backing down or giving up too soon.
Dominating the conversation instead of listening well or allowing space for criticism.	Being fully engaged in the give-and-take of reason-giving.	Believing or being persuaded too easily, through fear or inexperience; being overly apologetic about your views.

Sometimes people are arrogant and obstinate out of pure pride. They need to come off as the smartest person in the room. From this pride, however, comes a fear of being shown wrong in public. They're worried about how they might look to others if they're shown to be wrong or mistaken. If they secretly think that their position is weak and unsupportable, they won't listen to others, they'll blindly reject things without testing them. These are not purely intellectual mistakes. Pride and the fear that flows from it can make a person blind, rude, dismissive, and culpably ignorant. Like Harry and the Hallows, the powers of reasoning are better used in the hands of those who are both humble and courageous.

That said, you ought not fall for a false imitation of humility either, lacking the courage of your convictions, not speaking up because you don't believe in the worth of your own contribution, or thinking that there isn't any real wisdom to be found and it's all just subjective anyway, so no one's view—including your own—deserves a spirited defense. That's also a recipe for never learning anything at all. A good place to stand is a place that acknowledges that you can get things right sometimes. Everyone needs to start somewhere. It's important to develop your views and voice. So have the courage to use your intellectual abilities. Even if they are still developing and improving, you have something of real worth to work with. At the same time, you shouldn't be afraid to change your mind when a change is called for. Have the humility to acknowledge that you will sometimes make mistakes or miss things that others have seen or need to expand your perspective.

V. Putting It into Practice

The following five-step process is a suggested pattern to follow, a pattern of practice that expresses the values we've been advocating in this chapter, represented by four *p*'s: the *purpose* of wisdom-seeking, rather than winning at all costs; a charitable attitude toward the *people* we are arguing with; the sympathetic consideration and constructive criticism of *positions* that differ from our own; and a character that rightly combines the *propensities* of epistemic humility and intellectual confidence.

We'll describe the process as a face-to-face encounter (in class, at a conference, or in conversation), but it can easily be extended to other types of interactions (for example, in responding to a text).

Common Courtesy. A small word of appreciation sets the tone for the rest of the interaction. "Thanks for your paper / for giving us this occasion to discuss an important issue / for taking the time to address this difficult topic." If possible, compliment your interlocutor first, without condescension, before you launch into questions or criticisms: "I really appreciated this insight / the clarity of your presentation / your obvious concern for this important matter / your work on this project / your presentation of a point of view I haven't thought about before."

Clarification. Make sure you've understood the view right aright. "When you said X, did you mean . . .? / Is it right to say that [this claim] is the main point of the argument? / If I characterized your view as X, would you say that I understood you correctly? / Help me understand why you raised the problem this way instead of in other terms." If you find out that you have misconstrued their view, step back and reimagine the possibilities before you proceed with criticism. Get more information from them if you need to in order to make sure you accurately comprehend the argument.

Criticism. Identify a controversial step in the argument, and state your criticism fairly and carefully. "In paragraph 3 / step 7 / the definition of X in your argument, I hear you assuming that such and such is the case because of . . . But if you assume that, aren't you going to run into the following difficulty?" Or, "I see a problem with paragraph 3 / the definition of X. If I'm right about that problem, here is a counterexample/difficulty that arises . . ." Or, "If you look at things from this different perspective, I think you'll agree that your conclusion here doesn't follow . . ." Don't be afraid to follow up or press your point if you are not satisfied with the reply. You can also loop back to the clarification stage if you need to.

Creative Reconstruction. If you are creative enough, you might imagine a way out for your interlocutor and suggest it. "If you added this nuance to premise 4 / altered the definition X in the following way, you could avoid the counterexample and end up with a conclusion very close to/ still sympathetic to your original position." Or, "If you scale back your claims in the opening section, you could offer a conclusion that more strongly criticizes at least part of the position you were hoping to argue against."

(Re)Contextualization. In a book review, letter to the editor, or conversational exchange, it is good protocol to end on a positive note—to go back to the big picture and remind everyone listening or reading of shared goals or common ground, or to express appreciation for what you have learned, even if you end up agreeing to disagree, or to summarize each person's conclusions so far before you express interest in what direction the conversation might go in the future.

In a face-to-face dialogue both parties are present and able to speak for themselves. In that case, you will have to be a good listener and not let your desire to be thought smarter or more quick-witted by your audience undercut your ability to consider reasons fairly and carefully. Don't be afraid to respond by saying that you need more time to think something through before you are sure about your answer. For example, "My first reaction is X, but I will need more time to think through what my considered position on that might be." You can also try a hypothetical approach, "If I were to make this objection or concede this point, let's think about what might follow . . ." If you are interpreting and evaluating a text where the author is not present—especially a historical text, say, of David Hume, who died centuries ago—you will have to do the work of both sides. You will have to offer criticism and then imaginatively construct a fair response. This skill can also help you learn to anticipate possible objections by others to your own arguments.

VI. Summary and Conclusion

The world is full of complexity and mystery. We desire to be wise, but we are not omniscient. Voldemort-like arrogance and claims to mastery of complete and final truth don't fit us very well. We know, and yet we know in part. If we can recognize and live with our limitations as well as our abilities, we will be more inclined to give everyone more room to grow intellectually, and we will deal graciously with mistakes—the mistakes of others as well as our own. As people with a variety of positions and perspectives, we need both genuine humility and the courage of our convictions. And like Harry Potter and his friends, we will do better when we find communities of inquiry that expect and support those virtues—communities like Hogwarts itself, minus a few magic wands.

Glossary

Analogical argument: an argument involving an inferential projection from previous, known cases of one type to cases of a similar type.

Antecedent: in a conditional statement, the first propositional subcomponent; proposition A in the conditional "If A then B."

Argument: a piece of reasoning, consisting of starting points (premises) and an inferred end point (conclusion), typically employed as an attempt to persuade others.

Base Rate Fallacy: The conditional probability of a particular outcome solely on a specific piece of evidence not including the base rate (prior probability on background evidence) of that outcome often differs from the conditional probability of that outcome taking into consideration both the specific piece of evidence and the background base rate of that outcome. Any inference that ignores that background consideration is an instance of the base rate fallacy. This fallacy is also sometimes referred to as the *base rate neglect* fallacy.

Bayes' Theorem: a mathematical probability equation concerning changes in conditional probabilities when new evidence is taken into account. Named after the Rev. Thomas Bayes.

Bayesianism: very generally, the view that beliefs and changes in degrees of belief should be in accord with Bayes' Theorem. More specifically, sometimes used as a synonym for subjective probability.

Classical probability: the view that probabilities are defined by the proportion of specific types of outcomes within the set of equally possible alternative outcomes.

Conclusion: the proposition that the premises of an argument are intended to support; the proposition to be inferred from the premises.

Conditional probability: the probability of one proposition being true given the truth of some other proposition taken as evidence for it.

Conditional proposition: a compound proposition of the form "If *A* then *B*." Sometimes referred to as a "hypothetical judgment." In a conditional proposition, the first proposition (following the "if") is called the antecedent; the second proposition (following the "then") is called the consequent.

Connectives: the logical factors that combine simple propositions into more complex compound propositions—e.g., conditionals ("if ... then"), disjunctions ("or"), conjunctions ("and").

Conjunction: a compound proposition of the form "Both *A* and *B*."

Conjunction Fallacy: The probability of a conjunction of two propositions cannot be greater than the probability of either of its conjuncts. Indeed, the probability of a conjunction of *contingent* propositions cannot even be as great as the probability of either of its conjuncts. Any inference that violates either of those conditions is an instance of the conjunction fallacy.

Consequent: in a conditional statement, the second propositional subcomponent; proposition *B* in the conditional "If *A* then *B*."

Contingent proposition: a proposition that is neither necessarily true nor necessarily false. Even if true, it could have been false; even if false, it could have been true.

Contradiction: a compound proposition that comes out false on every line of its truth table; sometimes also a simple proposition that cannot be true due to an internal inconsistency.

Counterexample: a case contrary to a general claim, showing that claim to be false. E.g., general claim, "All swans are white"; counterexample, the black swans of Australia. Counterexamples to proposed necessary truths can be real or imagined.

Counterfactual: generally, a conditional in the subjunctive mood – *Were A true, then B would be true.* Such conditionals are also referred to as subjunctive conditionals, counterfactual conditionals, or contrary-to-fact conditionals. Despite the terminology ("*counter*-factual" and "*contrary*-to-fact,"), in philosophical contexts these labels are routinely applied to any conditional in the subjunctive mood, whether or not the antecedent is false.

Deductive argument: an argument in which the premises are intended to give logically conclusive support to the conclusion.

Deductivism: the conception of science according to which scientific theories and results consist of proofs generated by rigorous deduction from such absolutely secure foundations as necessarily true axioms and the like.

Disjunction: a compound proposition of the form "Either *A* or *B*."

Enthymeme: an argument with one or more unstated premises, or an unstated conclusion.

Enumerative induction: an argument involving an inferential projection from previous, known cases of some type to other cases of the same type. Also sometimes referred to as *inductive generalization* or simply *induction*.

Epistemic values: normative criteria for evaluating theories; taken to constitute evidence for the truth of a theory.

Explanandum: the purported fact, truth, phenomenon, or principle being explained by an explanation.

Explanans: the purported facts, truths, phenomena, or principles constituting the explanation of the *explanandum*.

Fallacy: an argument that is rhetorically or psychologically persuasive but otherwise defective. Fallacies are typically categorized either as formal or as informal fallacies.

Falsificationism: a view of scientific inference associated with Karl Popper, according to which theories cannot be confirmed, but can be disconfirmed by the falsehood of their predictions.

Form: the pattern of logical relationships among the components of an argument. Also sometimes referred to as an argument's "structure."

Formal fallacy: a fallacious argument whose logical defect lies in its logical form; can be identified simply on the basis of its logical form.

Frequentism: the view that probabilities are defined by the relative proportion of or limiting frequency of the phenomena in question within the relevant collections, populations, groups, etc.

Gambler's Fallacy: No specific rate of occurrences or absence of occurrences in the outcomes in a sequence of probabilistically independent events can have any effect on the probability of specific future outcomes in that sequence. For instance, if a coin is in fact genuinely fair, then even a string of 15 straight heads does not increase the probability of the next flip being tails. Any inference that violates that principle is an instance of the gambler's fallacy.

Hypothetico-deductivism: a view of scientific inference according to which confirmation of a theory is provided by the theory's predictions being true.

Inductive argument: see *enumerative induction*; can also refer to any nondeductive argument.

Inductivism: the view of scientific inference according to which scientific theories are generated and established by logical, inductive means from collections of empirical data.

Inference: the mental move we make from the premises of an argument to its conclusion.

Inference to the best explanation (IBE): the view that under certain conditions we are rationally warranted in inferring that the best of our available alternative explanations is true.

Informal fallacy: a fallacious argument whose defect is not merely a matter of logical form; an informal fallacy typically cannot be identified simply on the basis of its logical form.

Invalid: any deductive argument that does not meet the conditions of validity; that is, any deductive argument whose conclusion could be false even if its premises are all true.

Law of non-contradiction: the principle that contradictions cannot be true, that no proposition can be both true and false simultaneously, or that nothing can both have and lack the same property at the same time in the same sense. Often taken as an essential basic principle of reason.

Logic: the study of argumentation and reasoning, distinguishing proper from improper argumentation.

Logically equivalent: propositions that necessarily always have the same truth value as each other: necessarily, if one is true, the other is true; necessarily, if one is false, the other is false.

Logically necessary: see *necessary truth*.

Logically possible: a proposition that can in principle be true; a proposition that is not necessarily false.

Logicism: the view that probabilities are defined in terms of logical relationships within precisely defined systems.

melissa8022@servetusnet.stu: e-mail address to which you are invited to send your banking information to help a particular student needing assistance with tuition.

Methodological naturalism: the view that scientific theories deal only with natural entities, processes, and events whether or not a nonnatural or supernatural realm exists.

Mill's methods: procedures first systematized by J. S. Mill for identifying causal factors.

Modal logic: the branch of logic dealing with logical necessity, possibility, and impossibility (plus extensions dealing with epistemic, deontic, and other logics).

Natural Kind: a category, type, or grouping of objects, events, etc. that is built into nature itself, or that nature "recognizes," as distinct from those depending upon human convention or decision. For instance, *proton* designates a category determined by nature, whereas *breakfast food* does not.

Necessary truth: any proposition that cannot under any possible circumstances be false.

Necessary falsehood: any proposition that cannot under any possible circumstances be true.

Philosophy: literally, the love of wisdom.

Possible worlds: imaginative conceptual constructions of possible circumstances, useful for thinking about modal principles and a number of other philosophical matters.

Premise: propositions, principles, purported facts, etc., that are intended to provide support for the conclusion of an argument, and from which the conclusion is to be inferred.

Principle of charity: the principle that we should treat our opponents and their views as we would wish to be treated—respectfully, sympathetically, and accurately.

Problem of induction: a set of difficulties in providing rational justification for induction, first forcefully stated by the 18th-century Scottish philosopher David Hume.

Proof: an argument that guarantees the truth of its conclusion by meeting two conditions: it is deductively valid and its premises all are true; in other words, a sound deductive argument.

Propensity theory: the view that probabilities are a measure of some objective property of individual things or events.

Proposition: a statement with a truth-value; a statement that is either true or false.

Quantifiers: terms or concepts indicating the range of specific claims or propositions, such as "all," "none," and "some."

Scientific anti-realism: in its most common form, the view that science does not aim to produce, does not achieve, and cannot reliably recognize, true scientific theories.

Scientific realism: according to its most common meaning, the notion that science attempts to achieve truth in its theories and, at least in principle, can succeed in that attempt.

Sound: a deductive argument that is logically valid and whose premises are all true. See *valid*.

Subjectivism (regarding probability): the view that probability values are to be defined in terms of degrees of personal belief, provided those beliefs conform to the axioms and theorems of probability theory.

Syllogism: a two-premise deductive argument, such as modus ponens or modus tollens.

Tautology: a compound proposition that comes out true on every line of its truth table; also sometimes a simple proposition that cannot be false because the predicate is already contained in the concept of the subject.

Truth tables: schematic tools used both for defining the standard logical connectives (the conditional, the disjunction, conjunction, negation, etc.) and for determining the truth-values of specific types of compound propositions. They can also be used to assess the validity of deductive arguments.

Underdetermination: the fact that empirical data do not entail a unique scientific theory that explains those data. No matter how large the data collection, there are always in principle infinitely many potential explanatory theories covering those data.

Valid: any deductive argument where it is logically impossible for all the premises to be true while the conclusion is false; necessarily, if the premises of a valid deductive argument are true, the conclusion is true as well.

CPSIA information can be obtained at www.ICGtesting.com
Printed in the USA
BVOW03s0949200913

331560BV00008B/29/P